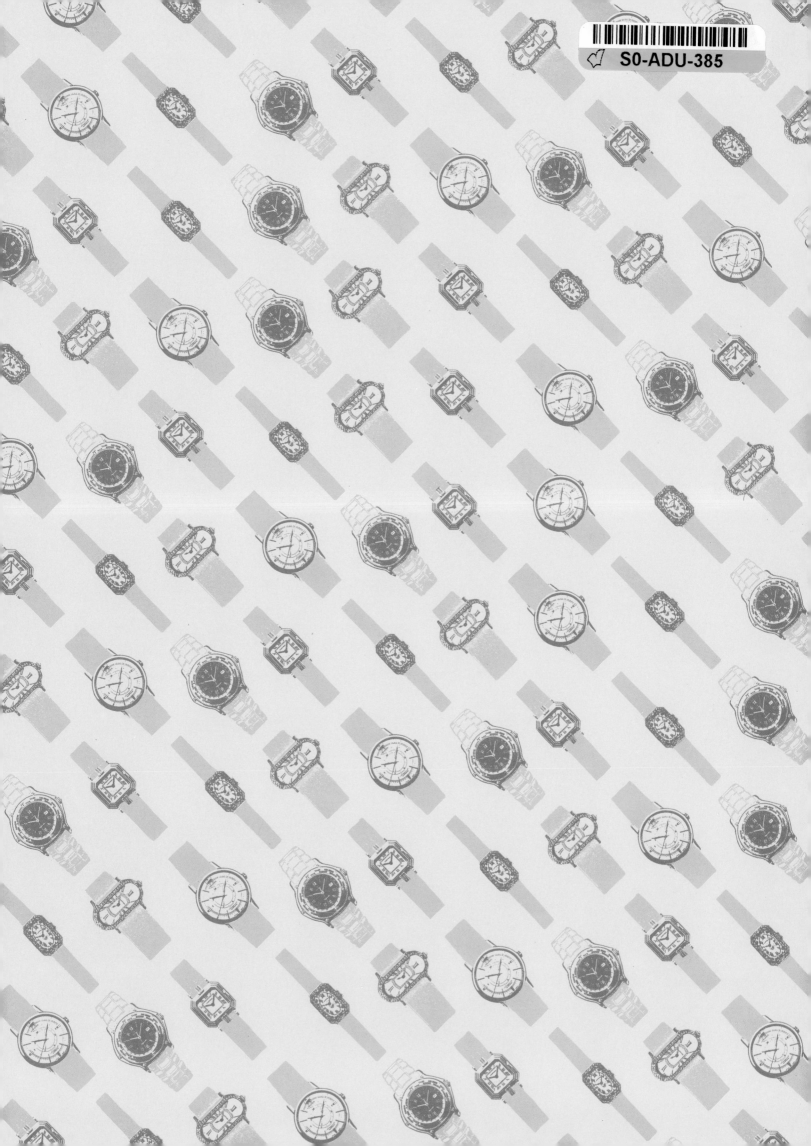

# WRIST
# WATCHES

# WRIST WATCHES

## THE COLLECTOR'S GUIDE TO SELECTING, ACQUIRING, AND ENJOYING NEW AND VINTAGE WRIST WATCHES

**Isabella de Lisle Selby**

Canadian Representatives:
General Publishing Co., Ltd.
30 Lesmill Road, Don Mills
Ontario M3B 2T6

9 8 7 6 5 4 3 2 1
Digit on the right indicates the number of this printing

Library of Congress
Cataloging-in-Publication Number
93-074688

ISBN 1-56138-431-3

This book was designed and produced by
Quintet Publishing Limited
6 Blundell Street
London N7 9BH

Creative Director: Richard Dewing
Designer: Peter Laws
Project Editor: Katie Preston
Editor: Ruth Baldwin
Picture Researcher: Isabella Selby
Photographer: Paul Forrester

Typeset in Great Britain by
Central Southern Typesetters, Eastbourne
Manufactured in Singapore by Eray Scan Pte Ltd
Printed in Singapore by
Star Standard Industries (Pte) Ltd

ACKNOWLEDGMENTS
Special thanks to Richard Leyens and Tina Baldwin.
Thanks also to the Antique Watch Co., London for
providing wristwatches for photography and to the
following manufacturers for supplying photographs:

Audemars Piguet ● Baume et Mercier ● Blancpain ●
Brietling ● Cartier, London and Paris ● Dunhill ●
Girard Perregaux ● Gucci ● Hamilton ● International
Watch Company ● Jaeger-LeCoultre ● Jean Lassale ●
Longines ● Movado ● Omega ● Piaget ● Rado ●
Raymond Weil ● Rolex ● Rotary ● Swatch ●
Tag-Heuer ● Tissot ● Vacheron et Constantin ●
Zenith

Published by Courage Books
an imprint of Running Press Book Publishers
125 South Twenty-second Street
Philadelphia, Pennsylvania 19103-4399

# CONTENTS

# INTRODUCTION

M an's fascination with passing time has been apparent for centuries, and over the years watchmaking has been revered as evidence of the natural dexterity of human beings. Long before production lines came into being, a cottage industry existed in Switzerland, France, and Germany where poor farmers, after trying to make a living from infertile soil during the summer months, would spend long winter days and evenings producing, cog by cog, the forerunners of today's wrist watches.

Although the first portable timepiece was supposed to have been worn by Marie Antoinette in the eighteenth century, the first true wrist watch was not invented for another century. Patek Phillipe is thought to have made the first wrist watch in 1868, but some say that a Brazilian named Alberto Santos-Dumont, who was conducting experiments with an "airship," mentioned to his friend, watchmaker Louis-François Cartier, how inconvenient it was to pull out his pocket watch while he was at the controls of his flying machine; when Santos-Dumont completed his record-breaking 240-yard flight in 1907, he was wearing on his wrist the first Cartier Santos-Dumont.

Since that time, few collectibles have been as useful in everyday life as the wrist watch, even though it has only one purpose – to

A B O V E **Early lady's Cartier wrist watch showing that the use of bright colors is not just a modern trend.**

T O P **Early twentieth-century production line high up in the Swiss mountains. The women were all very young and were closely supervised by the paternal figure in the background.**

LEFT **Contemporary Dunhill watch. The design shows the renewed interest in old styles.**

ABOVE **1990 Swatch Chronograph. This model was an immediate sell-out when first introduced.**

measure the passing of time. Wrist watches have become available for all occasions, made from materials as diverse as plastic and precious gold, incorporating works of art, or with novelty faces. There is a design to suit everyone.

The aim of this book is not to tell you what to collect, but rather to help you decide for yourself by showing you the variety of watches available. The focus of your collection might be the date of production, materials used, or the functions of the watch; or you could base it on a theme, such as military watches. The following pages will help you decide which way you want your collection to grow and to help you in your search for that elusive piece. Some watches have their place in history, others are linked to great sports events: this book will help you through the collecting maze and point out some of the pitfalls. However, whatever the motivation for your collection, you should start with pieces that please you and arouse your interest – a purchase based on price or rarity alone may be regretted.

A wrist watch collection has one advantage over most others in that you can wear your collection on a daily basis, swapping your watch in accordance with your mood, mode of dress, or the occasion. By reading, observing, and visiting museums, stores, and auctions, you will gradually expand your knowledge. Once the learning process has started, it will continue naturally until both experience and instinct are your guide. As your confidence in your own judgment grows, you will begin to look further afield, daring to buy the piece that is a little bit special and learning to trust your developing "feel" for what is good.

ABOVE **Le Crash by Cartier. Classics do not all have to take the same shape; a watch movement can fit into many shapes.**

# WHAT MAKES A WRIST WATCH TICK?

A B O V E **Zenith automatic movement. The plate bearing the manufacturer's name is the rotor which provides the power to the mainspring.**

On the market today there are three basic watch movements: hand-wound, automatic, and quartz. Hand-winding and automatic are jointly referred to as mechanical. It is important to know which is which, as a hand-wound watch will not start when shaken, but most good automatics will start when wound.

## THE MECHANICALS

The hand-wound wristwatch is, of course, the direct descendant of the key-wound pocket watch which, in the course of its natural evolution, acquired a winding knob or, as it is more properly known, a crown and stem.

The automatic movement has quite a long history, too: it was first recorded in 1770, and in 1780 the pedometer movement was first mentioned. A watch with an automatic movement is wound when the wearer's movement causes a weighted segment or rotor to pivot on itself.

It was an Englishman, John Harwood, who was responsible for the first automatic wrist watch. He began experimenting in London in 1917 and applied for a Swiss patent in 1923. The wrist watch he perfected was unusual even by today's standards: as it did not have a crown, it could be set only by turning the bezel (the metal frame holding the watch glass), and it had to be shaken to be wound.

 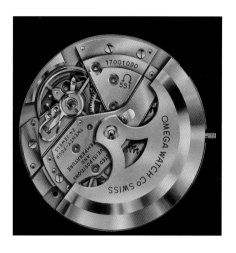

Prior to this, all wrist watches were hand-wound. Harwood wrist watches were manufactured in Switzerland until the early 1930s, when the company went bankrupt.

## THE ELECTROMECHANICALS

The advent of miniature batteries for hearing aids in the 1950s inspired a French company, LIP, and an American manufacturer, Hamilton, to join forces for research purposes, and as a result of their efforts, the first electric wrist watches were made available in 1957. These models were large, ugly, and not very popular – with one exception, which was to prove a commercial success, the Accutron. Created by a Swiss electronics engineer and with an accuracy of 99.9977 percent, it was issued with the first-ever guarantee of accuracy for a wrist watch by its manufacturer, Bulova. However, before Bulova was able to elaborate on the idea of the Accutron, the public's interest waned, and the concept of the electromechanical wrist watch was abandoned, having filled the gap between the mechanicals and the revolutionary quartz movement.

## THE FIRST QUARTZ WRIST WATCH

Quartz clocks had been in existence for some time before quartz watches. In the 1960s, thanks to miniaturization, electronics engineers in both Japan and Switzerland were working toward the first quartz wrist watch, and finally in 1968, both countries had prototypes. These, when submitted to rigorous laboratory testing, proved to have a remarkably small margin of error: only two seconds per day. Unfortunately, as with their predecessor, the electromechanical wrist watch, they were ugly to look at and

THIS AMAZING WATCH
WINDS ITSELF!

NEW as the hour and sound as Big Ben. The very latest in watches—the Harwood. Wearing winds it. Dust and damp cannot enter. The movement is of the best. Ask to see it at any high-class Jeweller's.

*Ladies and Gents Wristlets in 9ct. Gold for 8 Guineas.*

HARWOOD
SELF-WINDING
WRIST WATCH

Guaranteed and fully serviced by The Harwood Self-Winding Watch Co. Ltd., Dept. W1 252-260, Regent Street, London, W.1

THE IDEAL WATCH ACHIEVED !

A B O V E  **A 1929 advertisement
for a remarkable British invention
– a watch wound by wrist
movement alone.**

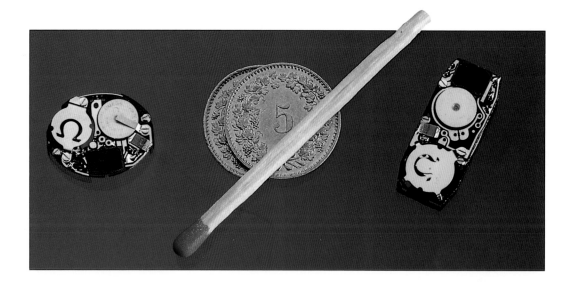

A B O V E **The size of these two Omega movements (long on the right, oval on the left) could be achieved only with quartz technology.**

A B O V E **A highly collectible Hamilton battery-operated Electric from the 1950s.**

clumsy in design. It now seemed to the manufacturers that the rational method of telling the time with a dial and hands should be superseded by something more in keeping with the watch's revolutionary movement. Liquid crystal displays (LCDs) and light-emitting diodes (LEDs) were extensively used. It soon became apparent that both these methods had a number of disadvantages linked to the display, not least the esthetic limitations imposed by their specifications. This, plus the fact that these watches could be produced very cheaply in the Pacific Basin, soon moved LCD and LED production out of the traditional watchmaking areas, and the end product was not deemed by jewelry and watch retailers to be high enough in quality.

The Swiss watch houses went back to the centuries-old tradition of dial-and-hand display. These, coupled with quartz technology, can account for some of the most outstanding-looking timepieces of today, whose quality cannot be dismissed, even by purists. It is now possible, thanks to the quartz movement which can be made very small, to produce ultrathin, very elegant wrist watches. These pieces, when fitted with a mechanical movement, were and still are in a price bracket which makes them affordable only by the very wealthiest.

All watch movements work on the same principle. The **time divider** which divides passing time into equal parts must receive power from a **power source**. This power must be transmitted from the latter to the former, so there must be a system for **power transmission**. Finally, the watch must **show the time** after the time divider has completed its task. The time appears either on a dial or on a digital display.

R I G H T **Front and back view of a Vacheron Constantin mechanical chronograph. The little needle at the twelve o'clock position on the back is for the regulator and permits fine adjustments to the timekeeping.**

A B O V E **Longines automatic Conquest from the 1960s. This movement is unusual in that it has a power reserve indicator in the center of the dial.**

## WATCH MOVEMENTS

|  | MECHANICAL | QUARTZ |
|---|---|---|
| **Time division** | Balance wheel | Quartz crystal |
| **Power source** | Mainspring | Battery |
| **Transmission of power** | Gear train and escapement | Integrated circuit |
| **Showing the time** | Motion work (dial train) | 1 In the case of the analog, or dial, watch, the stepping motor moves the hands on the dial. 2 For digital watches, the impulses control the liquid crystals or the light-emitting diodes. |

The mainspring of a mechanical watch will be tightened either by the turning of the crown on a hand-wound watch or by the swinging action of the rotor for an automatic.

A watch movement should be treated with the respect that the care of its manufacture warrants.

ABOVE **Omega Sapphette, 1955. This takes its name from the watch crystal cut from a special sapphire and which is faceted like a diamond.**

## OTHER WRIST WATCH COMPONENTS

### CRYSTAL

One of three materials is traditionally used for the crystal or glass dial cover: plexiglass, crystal (which is in fact quartz crystal), and synthetic sapphire. The third material has the same molecular structure as a natural sapphire, but has been produced in a laboratory. It is by far the most expensive to produce and is therefore used only on the higher-quality pieces or those watches made to withstand rough sports usage. The sapphire glass is scratch-resistant, but beware – nothing is totally scratchproof and, if you hit it hard enough, it will still break! Older sports watches tend to come with a plexiglass crystal as, until recently, it was not possible to shape the sapphire glass into anything but a level surface, which was unsuitable for some sports watches. Quartz mineral crystal, which is somewhere between plexiglass and sapphire crystal in strength, is used on many "everyday" watches you come across.

### MATERIALS

Disregarding any precious stones which may be present on a watch case or bracelet, the list of materials used by the watchmaking industry both past and present is as extensive as it is varied. Gold has been used in fine pieces since the beginning. Most versatile of

BELOW **Early lady's Cartier wrist watch with a pearl bezel. Pearls are fairly rare on watches.**

A B O V E **Large chronograph (1³⁄₅ x 1³⁄₅ inches) produced by Longines in the late 1960s. This model has the peculiarity of calculating time in tenths of a second.**

A B O V E **The RockWatch range was launched by Tissot in 1985; these watch cases are made of mother-of-pearl.**

A B O V E **Such was the success of the Memovox that Jaeger-LeCoultre carried the design over well into the 1960s. This one is hand-wound and was made in 1964.**

metals, it is used in both heavy sports watches and tiny elegant cocktail pieces. Surface scratches may be polished out; stones may be set into it; its color can be changed with the addition of other metals; and its value may be higher or lower according to the carat weight. The finish can be enameled, left highly polished, or be brushed.

## WHAT LOOKS LIKE GOLD...

Rolled gold was used widely prior to the 1960s, before technology made gold plating a better proposition – indeed, today's techniques have enabled some manufacturers to set a high standard of durability. Rolled gold is achieved by placing a layer of base metal between two thin layers of gold and running the resulting "sandwich" between a set of rollers (hence the name "rolled gold"), bonding the three layers together. Gold plate is made by putting a piece of base metal into an acid bath in which gold particles have been suspended and passing an electric current through: this bonds the gold onto the base metal. It is not always easy to differentiate between the two materials, though most gold plate has a slightly "harder" shine when given a polished finish.

Silver has also been employed in the manufacture of wrist watches, but not nearly so extensively as stainless steel. The latter

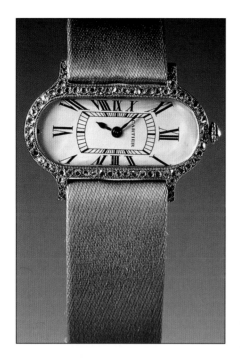

L E F T **Very early Cartier wrist watch on a satin strap. The time was meant to be read with the wrist held straight up rather than across the body.**

metal is the material most commonly used for sports watches both old and new, with or without the addition of gold or gold plating. Stainless steel is virtually unalterable, and it is possible to find early wrist watches made of steel which show remarkably few signs of wear and tear.

Other materials used in the more contemporary pieces include several organic materials: pieces of rock, slabs of shell, and even wood. Man-made materials include not just steel, but also ceramics, tungsten carbide, strontium titanite, fiberglass, and plastic. The Rado watch company, in particular, has done a lot of work experimenting with new materials; and the resulting pieces are outstanding in design and durability, combining as they do both style and strength.

## STRAPS AND BRACELETS

When a wrist watch is made, either a strap or bracelet is incorporated into the original design, the choice depending on the intended use of the watch. Although earlier pieces usually had leather straps, with extensions for wearing over sports wear, metal bracelets soon followed because they were more durable or, for dress watches, more stylish. A fine gold bracelet would be used to emphasize the elegance of the watch itself. Some ladies' watches had ribbon straps; naturally, very few of these models retain the original strap.

Logically, if the metal bracelet is the original, it will be of the same material (or combination of materials) as the watch case. It will probably be stamped with the watch manufacturer's name or logo. If a leather strap is used, check the buckle: again, if it is the original, it will have some identifying marks on it.

It is very important to look carefully at the strap or bracelet when buying a vintage wrist watch, mainly, of course, from the

A B O V E **Another very early Cartier wrist watch for ladies. The "bootlace" strap is typical of the period (c. 1926).**

A B O V E **A stainless steel, Midi size, Rolex oyster c. 1940–45. This waterproof watch was patented in 1925.**

R I G H T **Water resistancy is an important feature of most sports watches. This model by Tissot is water-resistant to 300 feet.**

point of view of safety (see page 72). If the strap or bracelet has deteriorated beyond repair or is absent altogether – a fairly frequent occurrence – try to replace it with one as close as possible to the original design. In some cases, the watch manufacturer may be able to assist you with information as to what the original strap or bracelet design was like.

·············· WRIST WATCH PROPERTIES ··············

## WATER RESISTANCE

Both the case back and the crystal need to be firmly in position to maintain water resistance in a watch. This is generally expressed in one of three ways: atmospheres (ATM), feet or meters. Since 1927, watches that are capable of being worn in the water without suffering damage have been manufactured. Since then, efforts have been made to produce watch cases that are more and more watertight and able to withstand higher levels of water pressure. If you have just purchased a watch and its water resistance is in doubt, get it checked – a rusty mechanism may spell the death of a watch, especially if it is left without expert attention.

A B O V E **9-carat gold Rolex dress watch with gold bracelet from the 1930s.**

## ANTIMAGNETISM

Apart from moisture, magnetism is the other main problem factor for a watch movement. We are surrounded in our daily environment by electrical equipment, some of which gives off a powerful magnetic field, and this can adversely affect the moving parts of a watch. Electric motors, loudspeakers, televisions, and video recorders seem to be the main culprits as far as watches are

RIGHT **What makes a watch interesting is a combination of design, technology, and history. On the right is pictured a rare Omega antimagnetic from 1925 with Breguet hour markers. On the left is a 1940 chronograph with unusual dial coloring to distinguish the various functions.**

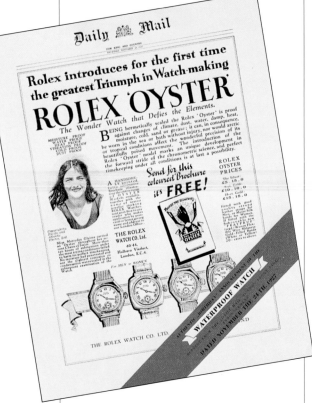

ABOVE **Rolex's front-page advertisement for their Oyster wrist watch patented in 1925.**

concerned because they are household items, but magnetic fields are ever-present outside as well as inside.

Magnetism will affect any watch parts which are made from ferromagnetic substances: for example, iron, nickel, or cobalt. The parts concerned with the accuracy of the watch are generally the most vulnerable. If the ferromagnetic metal in the movement comes into contact with a magnetic field, it will become magnetized and will try to realign itself, obviously affecting the working order of the whole mechanism and, in some instances, even causing the watch to stop completely.

The International Watch Company (IWC) of Schaffhausen, Switzerland, has done much research into antimagnetism. More than fifty years ago, IWC's technicians realized that if the whole watch movement were housed in a jacket which conducted magnetic fields, it would prevent the buildup of magnetic forces inside the movement. This jacket consists of a ring, a base, and the dial of the watch itself, which is made of antimagnetic soft iron. The company's flagship piece in this line is the Superantimagnetic Ingenieur. This watch, still in production at the time of writing, is worth having in any collection; the alloy used to make the antimagnetic jacket is no longer available, and production must soon cease.

# INTERESTING AND COMPLICATED MOVEMENTS

The primary function of watches is, of course, to tell the time. They do, however, do a lot of other things which can be used as criteria for a collection. Be it quartz or automatic, a complicated movement can only add to the intrinsic value of a watch, as well as having visual appeal. Fashions and fads may come and go in the watchmaking industry as in any other business, and in the late 1980s the public was crying out for moonphase wrist watches, not realizing that these, in a variety of forms, had been around for a number of years. Because of this craze, older pieces with moonphases and other complicated movements fetched record prices in the international auction rooms.

The collector's main concern is the beauty of the wrist watch itself, the hours of labor that have gone into creating it, and the dedication of watchmakers past and present whose thirst for knowledge made them look further and further into the possibilities of their craft. Such watches need not be prohibitively expensive, for with care and research it is possible to find some very interesting pieces at reasonable prices. This chapter is designed to help you recognize what you are looking at when you encounter it, rather than simply staring at a watch face and seeing a mass of hands and dials without having any idea as to their function and how to use them.

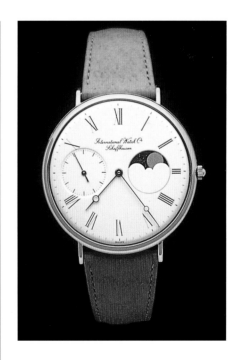

A B O V E **Pocket Watch on a Strap: unusual moonphase by International Watch Company. The second hand is at nine o'clock, and the moonphase indicator at three o'clock.**

When you have bought a watch with a complicated movement, handle the mechanism with care, especially when no instructiions are available; do not attempt to adjust it or set the various displays until you are sure that you know what you are doing. If necessary, find an expert and ask for explanations. In fact, although the watch may look very complicated, this is rarely the case, and once you have mastered the basic technique you will find that there are very few variations.

····················· THE WORLD TIMERS ·····················

With the increase in travel for both business and pleasure, it has become more important to have a watch on which the different time zones can be seen at a glance. This is also true for the business person who works with communications networks spanning the world. The principle of time-zone movement is quite simple: a rotating disk or interior bezel is marked with the name of a major city from each of the twenty-four time zones and an extra set of hands or another dial will track the time of the chosen zone. For a

A B O V E **Rectangular-shaped moonphase by Jaeger-LeCoultre, dating from 1949. Rectangular moonphases are comparatively rare.**

L E F T **A world timer by Patek Phillipe.**

long time, there have been watches capable of giving the time in two different time zones and even keeping track of two different dates. Of course, in the case of quartz movements, all these functions are spectacular in themselves. For an automatic movement, the difficulty lies in fitting in the extra bezels or dials plus the additional set of hands, together with a date window or dial, without making the watch very awkward to operate and at the same time keeping the buttons and winders to a minimum. The finer the manufacture of these movements, the thinner the movement will be; after all, these are not necessarily sports watches, and a certain degree of elegance is required.

ABOVE **Contemporary minute repeater by Blancpain in 18-carat yellow gold. The overall simplicity hides a very sophisticated movement.**

ABOVE **Contemporary world timer from Ebel. It is self winding and has a 40 hour power reserve.**

#### POWER RESERVE

The *réserve de marche*, or power reserve, is a feature found on some automatic wrist watches, sometimes paired with another feature such as a world timer, but frequently by itself. The power reserve indicates how many hours the watch will run if left untouched. The power reserve is generally shown by a single hand running over a scale numbered either from 1 to 36 or from 1 to 48, depending on the type of movement.

#### MINUTE REPEATERS

A minute repeat movement is the only one which tells the time by sound, and it first appeared in wrist watches at the beginning of the twentieth century. At the push of a button, the watch can be set to strike the hours, quarter-hours, and minutes. This is possible through a complex mechanical memory, the creation of which combines the watchmaker's art with that of the metallurgist, whose skills are needed for the manufacture of the hammers and gongs. There must be at least two different tones available, in order to differentiate between hours and quarter-hours, for instance. The idea behind this type of movement is simple: before the advent of luminous paint, it was not possible to tell the time in the dark visually, so another method had to be found – hence the minute repeater. A pioneering company in this field is Audemars Piguet, which claims to have produced the smallest minute repeater movement in the world. Audemars Piguet is also unusual in that it produces a rectangular minute repeater, which certainly adds to the collectibility value.

#### ALARM WRIST WATCHES

As with the minute repeater, the problems of making an alarm wrist watch with an automatic movement are not just horological, but also metallurgic. Unlike in a quartz movement, where an electronic sound can easily be produced, there must be metal striking metal to produce a sound.

One of today's most famous alarm wrist watches is surely the Grand Reveil by Jaeger-LeCoultre. A most interesting feature is the alloy used for its gong, which dates back to the Chinese Bronze Age, when it was well known for producing a clear and pure sound. This gong is kept separate from the movement so that its vibrations will not have a detrimental effect. For Jaeger-LeCoultre,

RIGHT **El Primero: moonphase chronograph by Zenith with an 18-carat gold case, part of a contemporary limited edition.**

RIGHT **El Primero: moonphase chronograph by Zenith with an 18-carat gold case, part of a contemporary limited edition.**

ABOVE **Early Memovox by Jaeger-LeCoultre, 1950. This one is made from pink gold and has an automatic alarm mechanism.**

the Grand Reveil is the culmination of many years' experience of manufacturing mechanical alarm wrist watches; another of the company's famous products was the Memovox wrist watch, made during the 1950s, which was the first automatic wrist watch to feature an alarm function.

A contemporary automatic alarm watch made by Maurice Lacroix, which combines a good sound with good looks, is worth looking out for because of the scarcity value of mechanical alarm wrist watches.

······················· THE MOONPHASE ·······················

The moonphase indicator on a watch dial can turn the banal into the special. Some of the movements linked to the indicator can be quite simple, merely showing a rotating moon which can be set more or less accurately. Others will take into account the lunar month, showing the twenty-nine and a half days with the various phases of the moon positioned accordingly.

Until recently, Cartier produced a moonphase movement (quartz) for its Santos range, which was, unusually, available as a lady's or a man's model.

It is comparatively rare to find a moonphase indicator on its own; it is frequently linked with a date display.

A B O V E **Omega Cosmic moonphase, 1947: the first Omega calendar watch indicating simultaneously the exact time (date, day, month) and moonphase.**

A B O V E **Cartier watch from the 1960s combining calendar, moonphase, and chronograph.**

## ···················· CALENDAR MOVEMENT ·····················

A proper calendar movement does not just indicate the date; in general it includes day and date, month and, perhaps, a moonphase. A quartz calendar movement will normally be programmed to take into account the different lengths of the months, but an automatic one will not unless it is a perpetual (a self-winding automatic) movement. It is important to make sure that the displays for the day/date/month are correctly synchronized; if they are not, the information will be incorrect.

The information is displayed by one of three methods: dial or windows or a combination of both. There is no set rule as to the position of each of these, so when purchasing a calendar watch, simply look for one that you find most legible and esthetically pleasing. Some people maintain that the more dials there are on a watch face, the harder it is to absorb the information at a glance, and this is perhaps true of watches where the design and final appearance have not been thought through thoroughly in the planning stage. However, you will soon be able to differentiate between a good dial design and a bad one that imparts confusing information or misleads the eye.

The first perpetual calendars are thought to have appeared around 1853. A perpetual calendar movement takes up where the

ordinary calendar movement leaves off. This movement should require no adjustment for leap years, thanks to a complicated system of wheels and satellite wheels or bearings, generally linked to the month display. In most cases, the watch's calendar display need not be touched until the year 2100 when, because of Pope Gregory XII's reform of our calendar in 1582 (whereby the year consists of 365 days and a leap year occurs when the year's number is divisible by four), either a minor adjustment will need to be made or a small part will have to be changed. In case of the latter, do make sure that the part is supplied with the watch!

### ··············· QUANTIÈME PERPÉTUEL ···············

The feature known as *quantième perpétuel*, which is often linked to a calendar or perpetual calendar function, indicates the ability of the watch to adjust itself to the specific number of days in each month: twenty-eight, twenty-nine, thirty or thirty-one. Again, the term relates just to mechanical watches; it is possible to have this function only if there is some kind of mechanical memory built into the watch's movement.

### ··············· PERPETUAL CALENDAR ···············

The perpetual calendar wrist watch sometimes comes with a year indicator on the face. This is a window, not a dial, to avoid the confusion of having yet another hand which would, after all, remain static for a year. If, when setting the date on a perpetual calendar, you go past the current year, the watch will have to be sent back to the manufacturer for resetting.

A B O V E **Contemporary quartz chronograph by Dunhill, including a calendar movement.**

A B O V E **Contemporary Blancpain *quantième perpétuel*: 18-carat yellow gold case.**

## GRANDE COMPLICATION

Only attempted by the very few, the *Grande Complication* is a combination of minute repeat, chronograph, and perpetual calendar movements. A piece with this kind of movement is a collector's item even before it leaves the drawing board and is the direct result of centuries of Swiss watchmaking tradition, combining today's technology with yesterday's craftsmanship.

Although the case will be made of the most precious of metals, this is one of the few instances where the movement is infinitely more valuable than the case. *Grandes Complications* first appeared in the second half of the nineteenth century, and all seem to have originated in the Vallée de Joux, near Geneva in the heart of the Swiss Alps which was then, as now, the center of the Swiss watchmaking industry. Their mechanisms were so precise that 0.001 mm could make a difference to the performance of the watch, aided by movements in which more than 650 parts were not unheard of. The wrist watch versions of the *Grande Complication* movement were first produced only in the late 1980s, but they are sought by international collectors and are probably not the easiest pieces for the amateur collector to find. It is very important to be aware of their existence; they are, after all, to watches what the Koh-i-Noor is to diamonds. Blancpain has produced a *Grande Complication* which includes a *tourbillon* (see below) and a split-second chronograph (stopwatch).

From start to finish, IWC's *Grande Complication* required seven years to produce. With such important pieces, it is not surprising that the instructions take the form of a full-size book and that each watch is individually hand-engraved with its own number.

The *Grandes Complications* are mainly available in simple unadorned cases of gold or platinum; with perfection inside, outside embellishments are not required and to add anything further would undoubtedly spoil the overall effect.

## THE TOURBILLON

The *tourbillon* is generally held to be the brainchild of Abraham-Louis Breguet, who applied for the patent in February 1798. It forms part of a mechanical watch's movement and relates to the accuracy. It is found only on watches of superlative quality.

The power from the mainspring is controlled through the escapement, the balance wheel, and the balance spring. When the

A B O V E **Rear view of the Portugieseruhr from IWC. This replica (one of a limited edition) of a 1940s watch was fitted with one of the slimmest pocket-watch movements of its time.**

A B O V E **Century slide for one of International Watch Company's complicated movements, to be inserted in January 2100 to give the watch another 300 years of telling the time.**

LEFT **The beauty of the tourbillon movement can be viewed through the skeleton back of this Jaeger-LeCoultre Reverso.**

watch is worn, the natural pull of gravity can adversely affect the rate of the movement so, to compensate, the balance wheel and escapement are enclosed in a cage mounted on a pivot. This cage rotates on itself, generally once a minute, to correct any shift in position caused by outside movement, thus keeping the rate constant. The *tourbillon* is often visible, being part of a skeleton watch (whereby the center of the dial is cut away to reveal the interior mechanism), or seen through a window on a dial or possibly through a glass back.

Obviously, such a sophisticated mechanism tends to make the watch a little more expensive. However, from a collector's point of view, it is well worth the investment. Such are the difficulties involved in the manufacture of a *tourbillon* that only the very large, prestigious watch houses will attempt it: Blancpain, Jaeger-LeCoultre, and Girard-Perregaux, for instance. Jaeger-LeCoultre have produced a Reverso with a *tourbillon*, combining the beauty of a Reverso case with the sophistication of the *tourbillon* movement.

# DESIGNS OVER THE DECADES

O utside influences have touched watch design like everything else. You will find that you will soon be able to date a piece just by glancing at it, as it reflects the style of its time.

Because early designs were usually linked to either wars or sports, they tend to have a heavier look to them, reflecting the style of the pocket watch, from which they are direct descendants. As the technology was first mastered and then perfected, movements could be made for finer and finer cases, until finally small, elegant ladies' pieces were feasible.

A B O V E **Longines lady's watch in 18-carat white gold with diamonds, 1915. The engraving around the dial demonstrates the quality of this watch.**

·························· THE 1920s ··························

After the quiet elegance of the Edwardian era came the "Roaring Twenties" and Cubism. Its influence was felt throughout the home, spreading into the sphere of personal adornment and accessories, and watches were not left out. The style was meant to reflect the new liberalism and leave behind the stifled ideas of the previous age. The concept that a utilitarian object could be good to look at was firmly implanted in people's minds and would influence the design of everyday wrist watches. Handsome pieces would no longer be reserved for the privileged few; prices were being made gradually more accessible, thanks to the advances of mechanization on the early assembly lines.

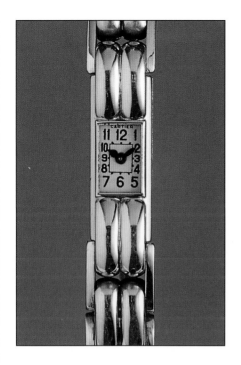

ABOVE **Yellow gold lady's bracelet watch from 1928. The movement is very small and the bracelet slim and elegant.**

### THE 1930s

The 1930s signaled the end of Prohibition and a new fluidity to the old structures of the previous decade. Surrealism was now the buzz word, and at the same time, the person on the street began to show an interest in sports. Watches for golf, such as the Reverso by Jaeger-LeCoultre, date from the beginning of the 1930s. Whereas men's watches were becoming more "masculine" in looks to complement their new outdoor lifestyle, watches for ladies' evening wear were growing smaller and more delicate in design, reflecting the new fashions.

An examination of the advertising of the era shows that manufacturers were trying to promote the idea of one watch for each activity or part of the wearer's life – one for sports, one for dressy occasions, and one for casual and office wear. This is probably partly because the techniques needed to make the more delicate-looking watches strong enough to withstand tough wear were simply not available at that time, and the cases for the more elegant styles could not take the pressures of vigorous physical activity.

*Pour vos courses, au printemps, prenez une LONGINES*

*Rendez-vous de chasse et de sport vous imposent une LONGINES*

ABOVE **Advertisement for watches from the 1930s.**

A B O V E **1932 – the year of the
Jaeger-LeCoultre Reverso. The
original models were mechanical;
this lady's version is 18-carat gold.**

R I G H T **Jaeger-LeCoultre
calendar watches from the 1940s.
Both show the date using an extra
red-tipped hand.**

A B O V E **Man's 1920s
chronograph with round dial in a
square, curved case by Longines.
The crown contains the
chronograph button.**

## THE 1940s

During World War II, all manufacturers' efforts were directed
toward supplying the combat forces, and civilians were generally
expected to make do with utility goods or with prewar products. As
a result, there are very few watches, other than military, from the
period. A few attractive jewelry pieces still exist, their small size
an indication of the difficulty in finding the materials needed for
their manufacture. Some of the watch companies of the time
actually stopped making timepieces during the war years, instead
supplying small machinery parts to the various government
agencies. What new designs there were were usually plain and
unornamented, on straps rather than on metal bracelets.

ABOVE **1945 Jaeger-LeCoultre Mysterieuse with white gold and diamonds. The small single diamond is the minute indicator, and the larger one indicates the hours.**

ABOVE **Longines lady's watch from the 1940s. The style is again elegant with the watch case tapered and set with diamonds in 18-carat white gold.**

## THE 1950s

After years of austerity throughout the world, materials were more readily available, and the affluent middle class grew in size. Designers began to set their stamp on everything from table lamps to automobiles. Couturier Christian Dior's "New Look" was also in evidence: after the lean years, this was an ode to extravagance. Watch design in those first postwar years slowly regained its momentum and became more adventurous, and with workshops now freed from wartime production, innovative movements began to appear.

In the late 1940s and early 1950s, however, there was still a lack of unnecessary frills, and designs were generally sober and clean-cut. On watches unadorned bezels seemed to be the order of the day, with plain hands and straightforward, functional dials. Ladies' watches were still, on the whole, very small and neat, with

RIGHT **A 1958 Omega advertisement for ladies' gold watches. The extremes in design of the years to follow are becoming apparent.**

*You Say a Thousand Unsaid Things*

When you give an Omega, you say a thousand unsaid things. Or, rather, Omega says them for you, and far more eloquently. So it will continue to do over the years. The high quality of an Omega movement is your best guarantee that your gift will be a lasting reminder of the happy occasion it is intended to commemorate. Unquestionably—Omega is accepted as the fashion leader in the world of high precision watches.

*Ask your authorized Omega jeweler to show you his complete range of the most recent creations.*

Ω OMEGA

*THE WATCH THE WORLD HAS LEARNED TO TRUST*

ABOVE **The Mysterieuse, 1948 version: the big watch manufacturers began to show interest in the more unusual designs, daring to move away from the austerity imposed by World War II.**

either bootlace straps or the ubiquitous "elasticized" metal bracelet. Although there was a newly emerging youth market hungry for consumer goods, increasingly fashion-conscious and influenced by a number of Hollywood stars such as James Dean, watch manufacturers continued to concentrate on the more established section of the population. The case design remained nothing more than a shell for the mysterious workings inside. But perhaps this was just a reflection of a certain starkness of design creeping in from the world of household interiors, where the use of synthetic new materials was leading to a total revolution in style.

Watches were still seen very much as functional items, except perhaps by the very strong names, with little or no fashion appeal to the young consumer, and the watch as a fashion statement for those from six to sixty was still a long way off, not least because the average cost of a wrist watch was then relatively high compared to average earnings.

RIGHT Lady's gold watch on a
leather strap from Cartier, 1970s.
The Cubism of the early 1970s is in
full evidence.

RIGHT Lady's gold watch on a
leather strap from Cartier, 1970s.
The Cubism of the early 1970s is in
full evidence.

ABOVE Cartier man's strap
watch of the 1960s with stylized
dial. Pop Art was just around the
corner.

## THE 1960s

It was only as the 1960s progressed that a more daring approach
was taken by the high-profile brands. With Op (as in Optical) Art
reaching its peak during this period, it was only natural that
something of its concept would filter down to such functional
objects as the watch.

Every design concept of the 1960s, in the watch world at least,
seemed to be "sturdy." Gone were the delicate little ladies'
watches of previous decades and, as the watch market found its
feet within the maze of new technological advancement and the
purchasing public grew more discerning, fresh ideas were
welcomed. In both ladies' and men's jewelry watches, colors were
used in profusion: turquoise, coral, and amethyst all featured. The
house of Piaget produced some outstanding watches during the
decade, pieces today displayed in museums.

It was also at this time that Omega produced one of its classics,
the Dynamic. Although it was not a jewelry watch, its design was
typical of the period: first produced in the late 1960s, with a thick
oval-shaped case and a very wide strap, it was made to be durable.
A production run of over one million means that the Dynamic
design can still be seen today, and the straps continue to be made
– proof of an enduring design if ever there was one.

## THE 1970s

The progress made in style and exterior visual appeal during the late 1960s and the 1970s may have been due to the fact that Swiss watch manufacturers were having to compete against the wave of inexpensive Far Eastern digital watches which were beginning to flood the international market. Technological excellence was not enough; the product had to look good as well as being functional in order to compete in a more and more crowded marketplace.

The 1960s was a decade of contrasts, with a budding consumerism on the one hand and a growing environmental awareness on the other, so it is not surprising that the watch industry as a whole started to lose its direction. This would contribute to the upheavals of the 1970s, when the coming of quartz led to a revolution in the trade, and extremes in design resulted from the earlier Op and Pop Art influences.

With the developing youth culture of the late 1970s and early 1980s, the rediscovery of consumer goods and the advent of the "yuppie" culture, there was an increasing demand for good-quality watches of fashionable design. The Swiss watchmaking industry showed its renewed confidence by bringing out more fashion-conscious pieces at prices previously reserved for the fairly conservative lines. Designer watches started to appear in strength

**A B O V E** **Omega watch of 1973 which won a design award (the Rose d'Or). Entitled Dimension 4, it has a silver bracelet and an amethyst crystal.**

**A B O V E** **Rado's Diastar 48, issued in 1973, the first quartz model from the Diastar range, showing the company's interest in unusual case materials.**

ABOVE **The watch as fashion accessory. This model from the fashion house of Gucci has a series of interchangeable bezels.**

to satisfy a label-hungry public, and fashion houses such as Christian Dior, Yves St. Laurent, and Gucci had watches designed to complete their "look" for the season. These pieces were generally made with gold-plated cases and Swiss watch movements. The fashion houses themselves obviously had very little part in their manufacture except to insist on stringent quality control. Such watches can make an interesting collection: as they were meant to have a very high-fashion appeal, the colors and materials employed may be slightly more adventurous than those used by the true watch houses. You can see the fashions changing through the watches, as the fashion houses tended to bring out new lines to keep up with the styles dictated by the catwalk.

ABOVE **This lady's Rodolphe, from the 1980s, the era of "power dressing," is smart and chic with a highly individual dial.**

## THE 1980s

With the 1980s came the "statements": the ex-hippies, now into their thirties, wanted something to show for all their hard work. World economy was booming, fashion trends were arriving thick and fast, and people had the money to keep up with all the changes. However, to show off all these marvelous new clothes and accessories and to impress on the boss that you were bright-eyed, bushy-tailed, and raring to go, you needed to be fit. To get fit, you had to participate in a sport – which meant that you needed a sports watch. The watch industry was quick to cater for this need, and by the late 1980s it was difficult to find a brand which did not possess a sports range.

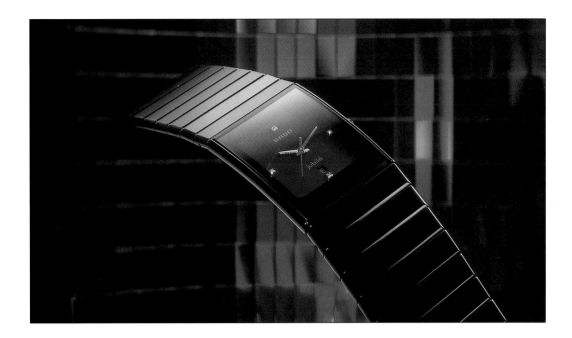

Nonetheless, to match their versatile lifestyle, people were still demanding slim, elegant "dress" pieces. The mid-1980s saw the emergence of some highly stylized pieces with strange shapes. For instance, the Sectora, by Jean d'Eve, had unusual hand movements dictated by the shape of the case. There was also a considerable growth in small watch companies cashing in on a fad for retrospective pieces using good-quality Swiss quartz movements in old-style shaped cases. Michel Herbelin and Emerich Meerson both made very attractive watches with good, sound movements, and some may still be found today.

·························· THE 1990s ··························

Sports watches maintained their popularity in the early 1990s, but there was an increase in models falling into the middle ground between the sports and dress areas, and some sports pieces even showed a few diamonds! The interest in reviving old designs had not died out, and copies of earlier watches remained extremely popular, either as true replicas or by taking the original design as the basis for a new version.

Designs in today's watch market, both new and replicas of vintage models, reflect an extraordinary range of ideas and trends. It has never been so easy to start an interesting collection; with many companies bringing out anniversary and commemorative pieces, collectors of old designs need not be subject to the pitfalls of buying and owning very old watches.

A B O V E **Art becomes function in the 1990s with this watch by Rado. Note the perfect integration of the bracelet into the watch case.**

A B O V E **The Color of Time by Arman, a 1990 limited edition by Movado.**

# ART WATCHES

The fine line between art and watch design was definitely crossed in the late 1940s by the American artist George Horowitz, a follower of the Bauhaus movement. This movement applied the theory that machine-inspired esthetics could be used for everyday objects. Horowitz's watch design, famous for its simplicity and still available today, features a plain black dial with a single gold dot marking twelve o'clock. Since then, several watch companies have maintained the tradition of asking a contemporary artist either to design a specific piece or to grant permission for one of his/her works of art to be incorporated into one of their creations. Most designs produced seem to follow the more modern expressions of art; they make most spectacular additions to any collection; but are widely sought.

For several years, the Movado watch company has made a point of commissioning watches as works of art from several major contemporary artists. One in particular, who made a sizable contribution although he died before its completion, was Andy Warhol, with his Times/5 wrist watch. Comprising five different photographs of New York as individual dials, this piece has five separate watch movements. It was made in a limited edition of 250; 50 pieces were retained by Movado, and 200 went on sale in 1988 for $18,500 each.

Another artist invited by Movado to design for them was Yaakov Agam, also a follower of the Bauhaus school, who in 1989 produced the Rainbow collection, which included not just a wrist watch but other timepieces as well, presented in four separate sets. These reflected the artist's interest in sculptural works.

Agam's achievement was followed in 1990 by The

A B O V E **An early art watch, this one from 1952 is by Longines. The enamel dial bears an astral theme.**

R I G H T **A Jean Lassale design inspired by Roy Lichtenstein shown on a background of the artist's earlier painting. The case is 18-carat gold with a golf ball engraving on the dial.**

A B O V E **Andy Warhol's Times/ 5, adapted from his design by Movado in 1988. This featured five separate movements and five different views of New York.**

L E F T **James Rosenquist's Elapse, Eclipse, Ellipse of 1991. The presentation case carries over the theme introduced by the watch.**

Color of Time, created by Arman, a neorealist painter and sculptor. Presented in a maple-wood box also designed by the artist, these wrist watches have paint brushes in lieu of the more traditional hands and swatches of color instead of numerals. The paint-brush theme is also carried over to the watch strap.

In 1991 James Rosenquist presented Elapse, Eclipse, Ellipse. Again, this featured several watches – this time three – with mechanical movements, made of silver and with a dark blue leather strap decorated with silver stars. The creation of this piece followed the artist's works entitled Welcome to the Water Planet: one blue dial, Ellipse, represents the earth as seen from outer space; Eclipse represents a meteor; and finally Elapse is an abstract concept of time. The piece is packaged in a pyramid-shaped box, an integral part of the concept.

Another design from the Movado company is its new art watch by Max Bill, called Bill-Time and produced as a limited edition of 99 pieces. The color patterns, both on the dial and the bracelet, are inlaid under tiny sapphire-glass plates.

Movado is not the only company that bridges the gap between art and design. The Jean Lassale company was responsible for the creation of a watch based on a 1962 painting by Roy Lichtenstein. This piece has an unusual 18-carat white gold dial, hand-engraved with the paintings' golf-ball motif.

However, before you aspire to such dizzy heights as the pieces mentioned above, consider the more accessible watches of other companies. These include Omega's Art watches, or even its Symbol range which features mystic symbols on the watch dial.

# JEWELRY
# WATCHES

A watch is very often the only type of personal jewelry that some people will wear, and it is important that it suits their personality and lifestyle. This does not mean that it has to be plain and uninspiring, since such a wide range of materials is available for watch cases. Stones can be set in the case, dial, bezel, or bracelet to turn an ordinary wrist watch into a dazzling piece of jewelry.

All kinds of stones, semiprecious and precious, from marcasite to diamonds, have been used to adorn wrist watches. The marcasite pieces from the 1920s and 1930s still exist in quantity, mainly in the form of the slim, elegant lady's cocktail watch, often with straps made of velvet or satin ribbon or leather no thicker than a bootlace. Before buying one of these watches, it is important to check the condition of the movement: they were often inexpensive to start with and may not have survived in working order. Where diamonds have been used, the quality of the setting and the color of the gems are important if the watch is very heavily set with gems, just as in the case of any piece of jewelry. The type of cut used on the stones should also be examined to help value the watch and to date it. Where the diamonds are tiny, a simple eight-sided cut is understandable, but if the wrist watch has larger stones, they should be of good quality, color, and cut.

A B O V E **Lady's strap watch by Cartier with white gold and diamonds, 1913. The size of stones above and below the watch case make this an important piece.**

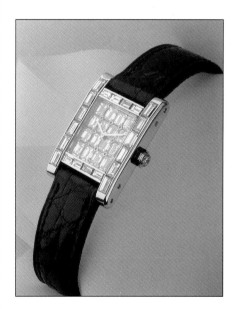

A B O V E **White gold and
diamond-set strap watch. The dial
is entirely set with diamonds,
leaving none of the dial plate
visible.**

Older diamonds tend to have a higher top section of the stone visible with a smaller flat top (this is known as old English cut), while the most modern stones will have a lower visible section, but a wide, flat top facet (which is called a table). When buying an older wrist watch set with stones, remember to check the setting, which may have become worn or damaged. A good way to check is to hold the watch next to your ear and shake it very gently – any loose stones will rattle slightly. Trying to match up a lost stone of unusual cut or color can be time-consuming, so any damage to the jewels must be considered when discussing price.

The case is not the only part of a watch's exterior which may be set with stones. The dials on both ladies' and men's watches can be made quite spectacular, with gemstones set in the positions of the numerals and dials made of slabs of colored stone or even rare woods, coral, or mother-of-pearl, either plain or tinted. Gemstones may be used not only for the numerals, but also scattered all over the dial in a tight "pave" formation, or at irregular intervals.

A B O V E **Unusual 14-carat gold Jaeger-LeCoultre watch from 1950. Diamonds are set outside the dial as hour markers.**

A B O V E **Dedicated to Gilda and to Rita Hayworth who portrayed her in the film of the same name, this watch by Jean Lassale has an 18-carat gold chain wrapped around the leather strap.**

Of course, while the appearance of a watch is being considered, why not alter the shape? Bangle watches, cuff watches, and watches on bracelets all lend themselves very well to embellishment with gemstones, and the possible permutations are endless. The shape of the case may deviate from the usual round or square form and may be heart-shaped, a half-circle, or even a totally abstract nongeometric form.

The beauty of the jewelry watch is very often related to the thickness of the case and the way in which it may curve to follow the line of the wrist bone. Although today most examples of this kind of piece are fitted with a quartz movement and sapphire glass, they cannot be made very water-resistant because of their construction. On older pieces, indeed, water resistancy may not have been a feature in the first place, so it is important to treat this kind of watch with the care that such valuable items deserve. They may be strong enough for daily wear, but not if that includes stripping down an engine or digging a flowerbed. Remember: diamonds and dirt don't mix!

The development of the extra-slim quartz movement in the mid-1970s really made jewelry watches more accessible and opened up design possibilities previously not considered. Many new companies with fresh ideas were founded as a result; for some, it was the start of a well-justified success story, whereas others with cheap and shoddy products were doomed to failure.

One of the successful companies was that of Raymond Weil; his Othello collection with an 18-carat gold electroplated extra-slim case, with either a plain black dial or set with Austrian crystals, marked a new standard for middle-of-the-line jewelry pieces. The Othello collection contained the slimmest quartz movement available in that price range and is well on the way to becoming a classic in its own right. It paved the way for Raymond Weil's first solid gold and diamonds wrist watch, the Parsifal, carrying on the concept of elegance which has been the company's trademark.

Jeweled wrist watches were among the first wrist watches, and stones from the days before modern grading and cutting often show subtle differences which can only add to the overall character of a piece.

Although jeweled watches for men are most definitely present on the market, the most imaginative pieces are ladies', which include watches hidden inside bracelets; slim, elegant, pretty

LEFT **Raymond Weil's gold-plated and crystal-set pieces. His technique of gold plating makes these spectacular pieces suitable for everyday wear.**

pieces; large bold "statements," and even sports watches made to qualify as items of jewelry.

Another relative newcomer to the jewelry-watch scene is Jean Lassale. Since 1975, when the company laid claim to the slimmest watch in the world, it has received numerous prizes, awards, and medals, but in 1985 it thrust itself forward with the Thalassa range. This featured highly stylized watches with models for both ladies and men, showing an artist's interest in design.

The Jean Lassale Company decided that a watch must be not only functional, but also an object of beauty, giving true pleasure to the wearer. With ranges given such names as La Passion, it is not surprising that Jean Lassale watches have a unique appeal. A company whose early efforts included a watch called Mata Hari can perhaps only be expected to continue with named models such as Scheherazade, and pieces which use lapis lazuli, diamonds, rubies, and emeralds. The Stella model is a strap watch with an 18-carat gold accessory clip set with diamonds and rubies. Jean Lassale has also launched something of a novelty, a boxed set of two watches, "his and hers," named the California range. This has a slightly more utilitarian look and feel, but carries the unique Jean Lassale design, and with their water-resistant cases and straps, the watches are ideal for those who require both strength and luxury.

The house of Piaget is another which makes very important jewelry pieces for both sexes. Its use of high-quality stones and the availability of the same piece with more or fewer gems allow a

ABOVE **Man's gold wrist watch by Longines from the 1960s, produced in very limited quantities. It has an engraved automatic movement in two colors.**

A B O V E **Important stone-set piece by Piaget with rubies and diamonds. The dial is pave set.**

A B O V E **White gold and diamond pieces by Piaget. The use of striking colors is typical of the 1960s and 1970s.**

flexibility in the price range which makes it an excellent brand for the collector to watch out for. This also applies to Baume et Mercier, which specializes in perhaps more delicate-looking jewelry pieces, including some beautifully crafted loose-link bracelets that are often attached to their watch cases with gem-set gold. Both brands have also shown a good availability in 18-carat white gold, which is somewhat unusual, but demonstrates the companies' understanding of public taste.

One general misconception about jewelry watches is that they need to be conservative. This has been disproved over recent years, not only by the younger companies such as Jean Lassale but also by the more established names such as Jaeger-LeCoultre, whose ladies' models such as the Rendez-vous and the Seductrice demonstrate that the company is no stranger to the craft of jewelry design. The Rendez-vous has one of the wittiest, most whimsical concepts that you are likely to find in a lady's watch, with an outer rotating bezel set with a diamond which can be used to mark the time of a romantic rendezvous better than a knot in a

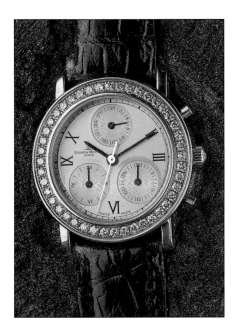

A B O V E  **Unusual diamond-set lady's chronograph by Baume et Mercier with an 18-carat yellow gold case.**

lace handkerchief and, of course, much more discreetly. The Seductrice, one of Jaeger-LeCoultre's more recent achievements, shows what can be done with one basic design. This again demonstrates the astonishing versatility that the use of precious stones lends to one particular idea, in this case a sinuous curved watch case fitting snugly onto either a leather strap or a bracelet made of the same curves of precious gold.

A jewelry watch need not be a major investment – there is something to suit most pockets – but you should make sure that the movement is still in good condition. Some people do wear old watches simply for their ornamentation value. If you own an exceptional piece, it is worth making every effort to get the movement working; in a few cases, it may be possible to replace the movement completely – though this is a purely practical proposition and does not add to the value of the watch.

Collectors should not ignore the more traditional watchmakers when searching for a jewelry piece. Rotary, Longines, Omega, and Tissot all have a long-established reputation as classical watchmakers and, as such, have all produced jewelry lines throughout the years, often endorsed in the past by European movie stars. Examples from the 1950s by Omega, with faceted crystals, are typical of their era and remain delightful to see and to wear. As early as 1930, Rotary produced some charming models using marcasite, some of them employing the concealed watch principle, which involved the piece of jewelry "becoming" a watch by flipping a catch.

It is hoped that the current interest in reviving older designs will spread to jewelry wrist watches and that you will be able to find more replicas of these fascinating pieces from a bygone era.

# FIVE

# Sports Watches

For most people, a sports watch is essentially a chronograph with a second hand, a stopwatch hand, and a minute-and-hour totalizer. However, there are specialized watches for many kinds of sport, including diving, flying, and yachting. These watches will probably have one thing in common: their size. Bearing in mind the degree of water resistancy required and the space needed for the extra movements, it is not surprising that sports watches tend to be that little bit heavier.

Many sports watches have a ratchet bezel, enabling the specific timing of, for example, a dive. On all good watches, this bezel is unidirectional so that, in the case of a blow to the watch in which the bezel is moved, diving or flying time, say, is shortened, not prolonged. If you intend to purchase an old sports watch and to use it for a potentially dangerous sport, it is of course essential to check the overall condition of the piece, making sure that the stated water resistancy is still maintained and that the ratchet bezel is intact.

All water-resistant watches should have their seals checked every so often, especially when they are used in salt water, which corrodes the inner sealing ring which may then need replacing. Water-resistant chronograph movements abound, but the chronograph cannot be activated or deactivated underwater.

A B O V E **Ocean 2000 by International Watch Company: Porsche-designed diver's automatic watch with water resistancy to 6,560 feet and a ratchet bezel.**

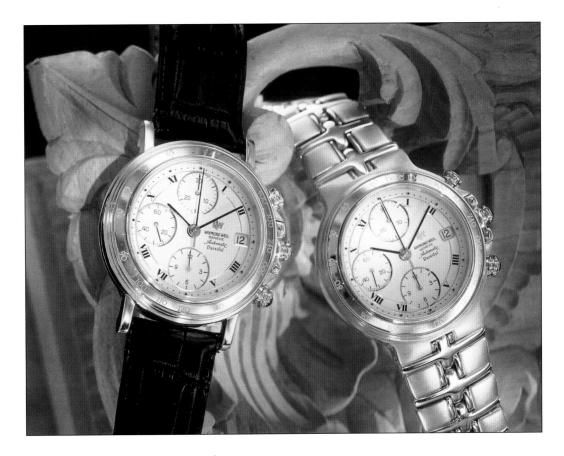

ABOVE **When sport meets jewelry: these two 18-carat gold chronographs from a line named Parsifal are by Raymond Weil.**

ABOVE **Breitling Chronomat: drawing used to demonstrate the slide-rule feature necessary to pilots before the age of flight computers.**

## BAUME ET MERCIER

As many watch companies have proved, sports watches do not all have to be ugly and ungainly. There is often no distinction between the functional and the beautiful, and many watches have surprising good looks but maintain the ability to withstand normal sports wear. These are available today both as current lines and as past successes.

Baume et Mercier is one such firm; its Transpacific and Riviera lines, both available in steel, mixed metal, and 18-carat gold, are fully water-resistant to at least 100 feet and are equipped with sapphire glass. The Riviera line has a chronograph among its many models, and the Transpacific is a chronograph line which, unusually, contains a lady's model. Continuing the Baume et Mercier history of chronograph lines, many of the company's 1950s models are still to be found today, and these also show the elegant looks which are the Baume et Mercier signature.

## BREITLING

Breitling is well known for its specialist sports watches. Many older models are still in existence, some of which have links with

L E F T **Breitling Aerospace, standard issue to the RAF's Red Arrows. This watch is made from a comparatively new metal, titanium.**

A B O V E   L E F T **Breitling Navitimer (contemporary version). The company continues its tradition of attractive utilitarian pieces designed with specific sports in mind.**

C E N T E R **Breitling Automatic Chronograph from the famous Chronomat line. This model for divers is water-resistant to more than 300 feet.**

important aviation events and with air forces all over the world. Breitling is no stranger to the chronograph movement, and perhaps its most famous in recent years, the Chronomat, is available in many guises. This automatic chronograph has a diving bezel and is water-resistant. Breitling also produces the Cosmonaute, a watch for the serious pilot, which has a slide-rule bezel and a twenty-four-hour movement.

The company supplies many aviation organizations, and its flagship chronograph, the Navitimer, is still produced today by the factory in Grenchen, Switzerland. Their precision and the ease with which crucial information is made legible are probably the main reasons why Breitling timing instruments have claimed a very important position on the instrument panel of many a legendary aircraft, such as the Boeing Clipper and the DC3, and you will often see retired employees wearing their official-issue Breitling.

The yachtsman is also catered for with the Breitling Yachtmaster, which has an automatic chronograph movement and five-and ten-minute warning zones.

ABOVE **1990s Cartier sports watch: the Diabolo with the revolutionary chronoreflex movement.**

## CARTIER

It is not surprising, in view of the growing interest in sports watches, that such a great name as Cartier should unveil its Pasha series in 1985, named after El Glaoui, Pasha of Marrakesh, who in the 1930s requested a watch that he could wear in his swimming pool. The Pasha is one of Cartier's most distinctive lines, available in either steel or 18-carat gold. Cartier has also fitted a revolutionary movement to one of the Pasha models, the Chrono Reflex; this is not just a chronograph but also a calendar watch, and its case seems amazingly small when the number of functions is taken into consideration. The Chrono Reflex has an ingenious system for indicating the number of years to go until a leap year, as well as the date, the month, and the hour according to the twenty-four-hour clock.

## GIRARD-PERREGAUX

Girard-Perregaux has applied its many years of experience to the production of both classic and sports chronographs and also offers a range of diving watches called Sea Hawk which would satisfy the most exacting collector. The classic good looks of its GP 4900, one of the few watches available in pink gold, are reminiscent of an earlier age, while the company's commitment to the future is demonstrated in the clean and sober lines of its GP 7000 series. In production since 1990, again using both yellow and pink gold, GP 7000 is a line of true sports watches with sapphire glass and automatic movements.

RIGHT **Two contemporary Girard-Perregaux wrist watches, one in steel and the other in 18-carat gold.**

## LONGINES

Since 1867, when Ernest Françillon opened the Longines factory, the company's name has been linked to major sporting events, with the commitment to precision timing that this entails. A manufacturer of marine chronometers needing to withstand the rigors of journeys to the Arctic and the Antarctic (not the least famous of these expeditions was led by Captain Bernier, when he navigated from the U.S. to the North Pole on his ship, *The Arctic*), as well as producing watches for sports from motor racing to cycling, Longines has been directly involved in great sporting events throughout the twentieth century.

## OMEGA

Omega's Speedmaster chronographs also have a long history. A hand-wound version was taken to the moon in 1969 – you can't have an automatic movement in the absence of gravity. With such an auspicious start, it is not surprising that Omega has kept up the Speedmaster series, retaining the basic idea but constantly improving and updating the design. Introducing a titanium and

ABOVE **Longines Conquest chronograph. This series was produced to commemorate the XX Olympic Games held in Munich in 1972.**

A B O V E **The Omega watch factory in Bienne, Switzerland, in 1895: a purpose-built watchmaking factory where modern technology replaced "farmhouse" production.**

R I G H T **1933 advertisement demonstrating the strengths of Omega sports watches. The models shown are stainless steel.**

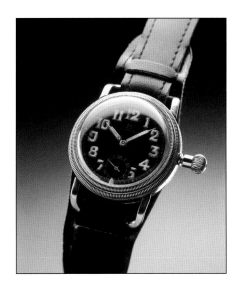

A B O V E **Omega pilot's watch from 1934. It has a revolving bezel with an arrow index for determining flight duration.**

rose gold Seamaster has been Omega's latest venture into chronographs, with a water resistance of 1,000 feet and a ratchet diving bezel. It is worth knowing that Omega first went underwater in 1934, so it is not surprising that the company has solved the problem of helium gas release in a novel way. Instead of having an open valve, it has perfected a screw-down crown at ten o'clock which can be opened if and when needed, letting out any helium while preventing water from seeping in.

When the Omega Speedmaster went to the moon, it was the beginning of a great tradition in sports timing for the company. Omega has produced a limited-edition Speedmaster chronograph with a run of just 999 pieces and available only in 18-carat gold. The survivor of a very impressive array of tests organized by NASA in Houston, Omega was the brand that rose above its competitors and, after that first moon mission, accompanied American

RIGHT **Omega Seamaster, water resistant to 6,560 feet, the Ploprof of 1970. This was used by Commander Jacques Cousteau for a series of experiments at 1,640 feet under water.**

ABOVE **Omega Speedmaster Professional. This piece was chosen by NASA in 1965 for moon and space missions. It was first launched in 1946; any model without the name Professional predates 1966.**

ABOVE **Contemporary Rolex Submariner with date, model no. 16610. Water resistant to 1,000 feet, rotating bezel.**

astronauts on several more sorties. Ironically enough, an agreement between the Russians and Omega followed.

To commemorate the twentieth anniversary of that very important date of July 20, 1969, Omega also produced an edition of 2,500 stainless-steel Speedmaster professional chronographs, each inscribed, as is the more recent 18-carat gold version, with the words "Apollo XI 1969" on the edge and bearing on the back "The first watch worn on the moon" and "Flight qualified by NASA for all manned space missions." It is worth remembering that the precision of these chronographs was so good that it allowed the crew of one space mission to make crucial calculations to establish navigational positions when contact with Earth was broken.

## ROLEX

One of the most famous diving watches of all time must surely be the Rolex Submariner, with an automatic movement, chronometer certificate, and water resistance to 1,000 feet. It is beaten only by another Rolex product, the Sea Dweller. Capable of submerging to a depth of 4,000 feet, this is, incidentally, the only Rolex with a date that does not have a magnifying bubble. The Sea Dweller has been produced solely in steel, whereas the Submariner has been produced in steel, yellow metal and steel, and all-18-carat gold.

## TAG-HEUER

It would be impossible to collect sports watches and ignore the importance of Tag-Heuer. Tracing its history back to 1860 and official timekeeper at the 1920 Olympics, Tag-Heuer has made a

ABOVE **A TAG-Heuer Formula I Chronograph – a contemporary classic among sports watches.**

ABOVE **The Rainbow, produced by Zenith in the early 1990s, containing the El Primero movement.**

remarkable comeback since the early 1980s, when it had all but slipped out of sight. In 1985 the link between the watch manufacturer Heuer and the group TAG (Techniques d'Avant Garde) was made, and Tag-Heuer has forged ahead ever since. Obviously, any piece that you come across with only the name Heuer on the dial predates 1985.

Most of the Tag-Heuers of today have a quartz mechanism, providing the precision demanded by competing sportsmen and sportswomen worldwide. Edward Heuer's interest in technological achievement led to many patents, the first, very early in the company's history, for a new system of water-sealing cases. The company's efforts were not limited to the field of watches alone: its expertise was also put to use in the making of car dashboard timers, and in 1942 it launched the Solunar, which showed the ebb and flow of the tides and indicated the times when fishing would be good!

Today the Tag-Heuer factory is still in a position to service most pieces bearing the old Heuer brand, either mechanical or quartz. Automatic Tag-Heuers are rare and much sought by mechanical movement fanatics.

## ZENITH

It would be difficult to discuss automatic chronograph movements without mentioning the El Primero movement by Zenith, used by other watch companies for their chronograph ranges. The El Primero is a classic, constantly revised and updated; it was first produced in 1969 and has been making a considerable comeback during the years immediately preceding the time of writing. It is thought by some watch enthusiasts to be the epitome of chronograph movements, having, as it does, many unique features. Zenith has recently produced a new range of El Primero chronographs, entitled The Rainbow.

With the current trend toward a healthier, fitter lifestyle, more and more people are taking up a sport. This has inspired watch companies, which have, since the mid-1980s, stepped up their chronograph production, and many fine new models have appeared every year to meet demand. When you buy a sports watch, make sure that it does the job for which you intend to use it – there is little point in buying a pilot's watch if you mean to take up deep-sea diving or yachting!

# MILITARY WRIST WATCHES

Collecting military wrist watches has many devotees; it is a vast, fascinating subject which enthralls a large number of amateurs and a few connoisseurs. Experience can be gained in many ways: by talking to members of the services themselves or by consulting watch companies' promotional literature, for instance. Books on the subject are few and far between, and translations do not always exist. The military wrist watch field is one in which hands-on experience is vital.

Not only do military wrist watches have interesting technological features; they also have historical connections which can again be used as the basis for a collection. Some enthusiasts collect only World War II infantry wrist watches, for example.

Military wrist watches first appeared during World War I, when it was discovered that it is difficult to shoot at someone while you are trying to check the time on a pocket watch. Also, by the time a pocket watch has been extracted, someone on the opposite side might have seized the opportunity to take a pot shot at you!

Military wrist watches seem to bear plenty of clues as to their provenance, but few direct pointers. Generally speaking, a pilot's wrist watch will have a center second hand, while an infantryman's or ordinary foot soldier's watch may have a second-hand dial above the six on the watch face. Pilots' wrist watches also tend to be a little larger, so that they can be strapped to the leg and used as navigational tools when needed.

In the U.S. during World War II, the products of the Hamilton watch company played an important part in naval operations. A special undersea Hamilton watch was made for the underwater demolition teams; for obvious reasons precision timing was a critical part of any mission, so these wrist watches played a significant role.

A B O V E **1940 pilot's watch by IWC. Fitted with a pocket-watch movement, it was meant to be worn over a flying suit.**

L E F T **Military wrist watches by Omega from World War I. Made in 1917, the one on the left was issued to members of the US Signal Corps.**

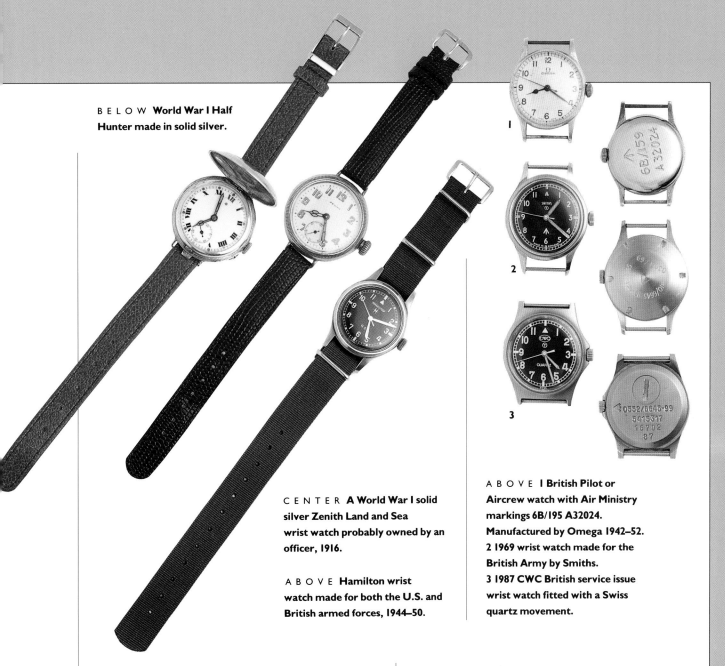

BELOW **World War I Half Hunter made in solid silver.**

CENTER **A World War I solid silver Zenith Land and Sea wrist watch probably owned by an officer, 1916.**

ABOVE **Hamilton wrist watch made for both the U.S. and British armed forces, 1944–50.**

ABOVE **1 British Pilot or Aircrew watch with Air Ministry markings 6B/195 A32024. Manufactured by Omega 1942–52. 2 1969 wrist watch made for the British Army by Smiths. 3 1987 CWC British service issue wrist watch fitted with a Swiss quartz movement.**

You may come across the World War I term "hack watches." One of the jobs of a plane's navigator was to give his crew a time check so that they could synchronize their watches, and this was known as "hacking." These "hacks" were often Hamilton wrist watches.

Marking on the case backs of military wrist watches will give a clue as to whom they were issued and for what purpose. "6B" may be found on pieces issued to the British RAF and to the crews of aircraft carriers; "W10" on British land army watches. American watches are often marked with a US Army patent and the name of the corps or division. WWW on cases stands for waterproof wrist watch. Military wrist watches often came with a webbed canvas strap and had black dials.

Many military wrist watches were and still are produced by some of the big watch companies, such as IWC, Omega, and Jaeger-LeCoultre (in very rare instances); others are produced by companies specializing in military supplies. Military wrist watch production is not confined to war time: contemporary pieces find their way into stores and auctions, and their provenance is easier to verify.

Not all the names found on military wrist watches will be familiar – names such as Smiths, which produced watches for the British RAF; CWC, which made both quartz and mechanical wrist watches; and Vertex, for instance. All are well known for their military productions and are ideal for the novice. Before making a purchase, make sure that you are buying a genuine military wrist watch and not just a souvenir piece.

# SIX

# CLASSIC COLLECTIBLES

A combination of many factors makes a classic watch: durability of style and design and a certain understated elegance, plus strength of case and reliability of movement to withstand years of daily wear. These qualities can be achieved only if manufacturers are prepared to spend time and trouble over their products – shoddy workmanship and poor quality control never make possible the durability required for a true classic. Unfortunately, it is not enough simply for a watch to wear well. Parts need to be available over the years, and straps must be found for strap watches if there is a special fitting involved. All this suggests some sort of continuity as far as the manufacturer is concerned. When you are buying a watch with such potential, remember that you will be wearing it for many years, and its appearance must remain pleasing to you. In this regard, lasting style very often equals simplicity of design and purity of line; anything too fussy will probably not remain to your taste throughout the years to come.

Some watch houses have specialized more than others in the production of classic lines. They have been making the same basic designs for years, with perhaps slight variations in the dial or movement. These pieces have achieved their reputation through their performance over a length of time, proving their strength, durability, and refusal to cater for passing fads.

A B O V E **From design to finished product, a classic never shows its age. This wrist watch by Cartier looks as good as it did when new in 1927.**

ABOVE **Contemporary Vacheron Constantin; the bi-colored dial adds to the clarity of the face.**

LEFT **An early Rado Diastar in which the use of modern materials contributes to the creation of new classics.**

## THE GREAT MAKERS

Audemars Piguet • Baume & Mercier • Blancpain
• Breguet • Breitling • Cartier • Chopard
• Corum • Dunhill • Ebel • Georg Jensen
• Gérald Genta • Girard-Perregaux • Ingersoll
International Watch Company • Jaeger-LeCoultre
• Longines • Movado • Omega • Patek Philippe
• Piaget • Raymond Weil • Rolex • Rotary •
Tissot • Ulysse Nardin • Vacheron Constantin

Blancpain, for example, despite huge pressure on the watch business as a whole since the 1970s, refuses to produce quartz movements and has, indeed, adopted as its maxim "There has never been a quartz Blancpain and there never will be." However, without going to such extremes, all reputable watch houses have a "classic" line, usually consisting of a strap watch with a plain gold case and either a white dial with black numerals or a champagne dial with baton markers, and available in versions for both men and women. These lines are generally manufactured for a number of years, discontinued, then reintroduced with slight variations to continue the original theme. It can be extremely interesting to locate the original of a particular series and follow it through to the present day.

A B O V E **Royal Oak by Audemars Piguet. This model has been available in a variety of materials since the 1970s.**

A B O V E **Contemporary Blancpain moonphase. Around the moonphase indicator are the divisions of the lunar month.**

If you can find them, old catalogs can be a valuable aid to this type of collection, as they show the name of each line and list its various characteristics. A classic line does not mean an uninspired appearance. Sometimes the most innovative designs can prove to be enduring lines which can be developed over many years, simply because the original concept was so good that no alteration was necessary to maintain its visual appeal.

### AUDEMARS PIGUET

The Audemars Piguet watch factory was founded in 1875 by Jules Audemars and Edouard Piguet, yet another with its home in the Vallée de Joux in Switzerland where it was, at the time, the third largest employer – with ten employees! Today, descendants of the original founders are still on the board of the company.

From its earliest years, Audemars Piguet established itself as a manufacturer of complicated movements, and in 1920 it was responsible for the smallest repeater watch, measuring only $\frac{5}{8}$ inch in diameter.

In 1972 came the Royal Oak, named after three Royal Navy battleships which were themselves named for Charles I's famous hiding place after his defeat by Cromwell. The design is of a quality that succeeds in emphasizing both simple and complicated movements, and its pinnacle was perhaps achieved with the automatic *Quantième Perpétuel* first produced in 1984 and much sought after as a major collector's item since that date. Not only does the Royal Oak design set off some of the most beautiful movements, it also lends itself to production in many different metals, ranging from the traditional watchmaking materials to that relative newcomer to the industry, tantalum.

### BLANCPAIN

Since 1735, there has never been a quartz Blancpain and there never will be – such is the motto of the Blancpain house and indeed, in 1735 when Jehan-Jacques Blancpain founded his watchmaking enterprise in the Jura Mountains, he established himself as a perfectionist. All Blancpain pieces still carry the undeniable stamp of craftsmanship visible at a glance; each order is the personal responsibility from beginning to end of an individual watchmaker, who signs the piece when it is finished. The Blancpain workshop, housed in a former farmhouse, is about as far from an assembly line as you can get.

A B O V E **Classic Cartier Tank made from 18-carat gold. This basic design exists in many forms. The simplicity of the case is well set off by the leather strap.**

A B O V E **Cartier jeweled strap watch. Note the unusual diamond-set design on each side of the case.**

A B O V E **Santos by Cartier, a 1930s version presented on a leather strap. Today's models are more usually sold on a bracelet.**

## CARTIER

In existence since 1847, the firm of Cartier is synonymous with outstanding quality. The company is responsible for some of the most beautiful jewelry ever seen and has been translating its experience of incredibly high standards into the art of watchmaking since 1888. In the decades that followed, Cartier has produced countless pieces, each more beautiful than the last, and for many reasons, classic collectors' items in their own right.

Continuing the tradition of quality that made Louis-François Cartier supplier to the Imperial Court of Napoleon III, Les Must de Cartier were launched in 1973. These were a variety of items starting with watches, but continuing with pens, lighters, perfumes, and so on, that were more a definition of lifestyle than a production series of utilitarian objects. Les Must de Cartier watches have has been continued from that date using the same basic case design, either rectangular or circular, but with the periodic introduction of a new dial.

The Cartier design team has shown, over the years, what can be done with a basic roman numeral dial while still maintaining the tradition of quality which makes Cartier such a great name. For instance, the numerals can be enlarged so that they virtually join in the center, or placed to run down the side of the case.

LEFT **These early Dunhills
reveal the popularity of the
rectangular case in the first part of
this century.**

ABOVE **This Dunhill, although
contemporary, demonstrates the
elegance of classic lines.**

## DUNHILL

Not all watch brands that have enjoyed lasting popularity belong to
a traditional watchmaking or jewelry firm. The company of Alfred
Dunhill, for example, that very English purveyor of luxury goods,
has, since it was started at the beginning of this century, produced
very fine pieces which still attract considerable attention today.
Their most famous designs include the Vermeil (1975), the
Millennium series (1982), the Elite (1986), and the Limited
Edition Dress Watches.

## JAEGER-LECOULTRE

When the first Monsieur LeCoultre settled in the Vallée de Joux
during the sixteenth century, in the process of fleeing persecution
by the Catholics in France, little did he realize that he was
founding a famous dynasty. This was to come into its own in 1833
in a place called Le Sentier, when Antoine LeCoultre opened up
his own watchmaking factory. Today, Jaeger-LeCoultre movements
and cases are still produced by hand in Le Sentier.

The house of Jaeger-LeCoultre has traditionally been
responsible for many "firsts." For example, in 1847 LeCoultre et

ABOVE **One of the first
Reversos by Jaeger-LeCoultre.
This piece from 1931 shows why it
has become one of the most
famous classics still available
today.**

Cie produced the first keyless watch mechanism, replacing the key with a crown winder on the side of the case.

Although not strictly to do with watchmaking but of outstanding interest from a horological point of view, the "almost perpetual motion" Atmos Clock was also the brainchild of Jaeger-LeCoultre. This unique timepiece is powered by minute differences in temperature; there is no key or electric impulse. The production of the Atmos Clock has continued since 1930, and an example is traditionally presented to visiting dignitaries by the Swiss government.

It is unsurprising that another of the company's products has shown similar endurance – the Reverso, first produced in 1931 and still made today. Combining the beauty and purity of line of the era of its conception with the strength necessary for the sportsman or sportswoman of that time, the Reverso, with its ability to pivot on itself to get out of harm's way, was a true classic in every sense right from the beginning.

## LONGINES

Longines has also produced classic collectibles, perhaps the most interesting being the Lindbergh line which commemorated the

A B O V E **A rare classic from the 1940s by Longines: 9-carat gold rectangular case and unusual grooved horns that cover the strap attachment.**

A B O V E **Late 1940s Longines in 18-carat gold with teardrop-shaped horns.**

R I G H T **One of the Lindbergh line of wrist watches in 18-carat gold. Its unique design was first thought of by Lindbergh himself.**

1927 crossing of the Atlantic by Charles Lindbergh in his airplane, the *Spirit of St. Louis*. This event gave birth to the Lindbergh collection in 1933 – the original sketch for the wrist watch was made by Lindbergh himself. Another of the company's successes in durability and strength was the Conquest line, a very sports-oriented design, but slim and elegant enough to rate as a classic; it contained a quartz movement, revolutionary in that it could be guaranteed an accuracy of twelve seconds per year, an achievement even for quartz.

## OMEGA

Omega has produced a number of collectible lines over the years, including not only the classic De Ville series, but also the more adventurous Constellation. For the more experienced collector, Omega's Louis Brandt line, all automatic, includes a perpetual calendar, a chronograph, and a plain automatic movement in 18-carat gold on leather straps. This series was produced to celebrate the company's founder, Louis Brandt (1825–79).

RIGHT **A hand-wound Omega from 1967. One of the first from the company's on-going De Ville series.**

LEFT **Rolex Perpetual Datejust
steel and yellow metal model no.
16233 with a sapphire glass and a
screw-down crown: a classic
suitable for sports wear.**

## ROLEX

Hans Wilsdorf, a name remembered by all watch lovers, was the
founder of the Rolex watch company in 1905. By 1910, Rolex had
obtained the first chronometer certificate ever awarded to a
wrist watch. The firm worked hard to improve the strength of wrist
watches, which were at that time rather prone to damage by dust
and humidity. By 1926, it was conducting tests which involved
immersing a watch in water for three weeks, and in 1927 Mercedes
Glietze swam the English Channel wearing a Rolex Oyster. The
company had found the solution to the problem of making a
watertight case with the invention of the screw-down crown in what
was, for Rolex, the beginning of a series of watches, each
guaranteeing water resistance to unheard-of depths.

Rolex did not confine itself to the production of sports or sports-
orientated watches. In 1931, a patent was granted for the Perpetual
mechanism, thanks to which, in 1945, the Rolex Datejust became
the first wrist watch with a date display on the watch face. Again,
taking the idea further proved to be no problem for Rolex, and in
1956 the Day-Date was launched.

It is uncertain which Rolex model is the most collectible, from
the earliest cushion shapes to the well-known Datejust. For many,
Rolex pieces represent the climax of the art of watchmaking, and
even for the non-connoisseur, their image is one of the ultimate in
luxury and desirability.

This chapter has discussed the work of a very small number of the
watchmakers which produce classic pieces whose fame and
collectibility has remained constant throughout the years. There
are, of course, many more, not all of which have achieved such
international recognition, but which are worth searching for
because of their quality, even if a little tenacity is required to
locate a particular model.

ABOVE **A highly collectible 9-
carat Gold Rolex Oyster from 1927
– one of the first waterproof gold
watches.**

# THE SWATCH PHENOMENON

In the late 1970s, while most of the world was gyrating around the dance floor to the sound of the Bee Gees and Boney M, Swiss watchmaking was sinking deeper and deeper into recession. On an international level, the economy was looking good, so there was a potential market for watches; nonetheless, the Swiss industry was suffering badly, with frequent closures and staff cutbacks. The Japanese, meanwhile, had eased their way into quartz movement production and were constantly occupied in perfecting their skills and refining their products.

Two important Swiss watch groups were equally affected by this growing crisis. Allgemeine Schweizerische Uhrenindustrie AG (ASUAG) and Société Suisse pour l'Industrie Horlogère (SSIH) – now combined as the Swiss Corporation for Microelectronics and Watchmaking Industries Ltd (SMH) – put their heads together and, spurred on by imminent disaster, came up with an extra-flat movement only ²⁄₂₅ inch thick. Called the Delirium, its production and development led the way to a simpler quartz movement costing much less than was previously feasible.

The new movement was ideal for a project already underway which called for a movement as inexpensive as possible to fit into a plastic case. The final producer of the watch (not initially intended to be sold as an "own label") would need only to specify the color

A B O V E **Keith Haring, Swatch Art, 1986: Modele Avec Personnages (GZ 100), Millepattes (GZ 103), Serpent (GZ 102), Blanc Sur Noir (GZ 104).**

required. After the number of pieces normally used in a quartz movement had been reduced from 91 to 51 and experiments had been carried out with various items such as Lego blocks and throw-away cigarette lighters for the molding of the case, Swatch was ready to be born. It had taken three years of intensive planning to produce a waterproof, shock-resistant, accurate watch made of synthetic materials with a low production cost.

At this point, it was decided that the new product would be marketed in-house. It was not enough simply to produce such a watch; the idea of a quality item made of synthetic material had to be communicated to the public, and for that a catchy, easily recognizable name had to be found. A New York advertising executive came up with the winning idea. The promotional slogan for the launch was to have been: "You have a second home, why not a second watch?," which resulted in S-Watch, and finally, by 1981, the name Swatch came into being.

The first Swatches were released to the public on March 1, 1983; there were twelve models and a maximum selling price of SWfr49.90. The launch was carried out in Switzerland, Germany, and Britain.

That year also saw the initial planning and conception of the Pop Swatch. Thus from a simple idea sprang one of the most innovative design concepts of our time, making Swatch one of the most collectible wrist watches. It is ideal for the beginner, not only because of its huge following (there are Swatch collectors' clubs in most countries – ask your local supplier for details), but also because of its reasonable price and visual appeal.

A B O V E **700 years Swiss confederacy, Flack (GZ 117) by Niklaus Troxler, Swatch Art, 1991.**

T O P **Yuri (GG 118), Igorts Swatch, 1992, Fall/Winter.**

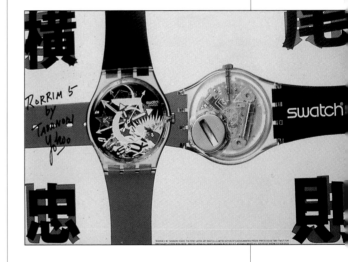

A B O V E **Tadanori Yokoo (GZ 107, Rorrim 5), Swatch Art, 1987.**

RIGHT **Blow Your Time Away:
Black Puff, Havana Puff, Royal
Puff, Petrol Puff, Cardinal Puff,
Swatch Specials, 1988.**

ABOVE **The original Swatch
Jelly Fish, 1983.**

·············· SWATCH COMES INTO ITS OWN ··············

From the spring of 1984, all Swatches produced were given a name
as well as a number, and with the first Swatch Specials the
collecting of Swatches may be said to have truly begun. The first
Special was the original Jelly Fish (1983), closely followed by the
1984 Olympic Specials.

One of the most remarkable Specials, but a series this time, was
the Puff series, which had as its theme "Blow your time away."
This was the 1988 Christmas Special; it was in 1987 that the
Christmas Specials began with the GZ 105, Bergstrüssli, followed
by the Christmas 1988 Bonaparte, but these were mere
preliminaries leading up to Christmas 1992 and the Chandelier,
the Christmas Special for that year. As an indication of its
popularity, when an outlet was set up in London's Covent Garden
for one day and allocated 1,000 pieces, Swatch enthusiasts from
all over the world lined up overnight, and by 4 p.m. on this one-
day opening the store had nothing left to sell.

The Christmas Specials are just one facet of the Swatch story.
There are also Swatch Chronographs, Scuba Swatches, Maxi
Swatches, Art Swatches, Swatch Automatics, the Swatch Pager,
and lately the "Swatch Musicall," a musical alarm Swatch
designed by Jean Michel Jarre.

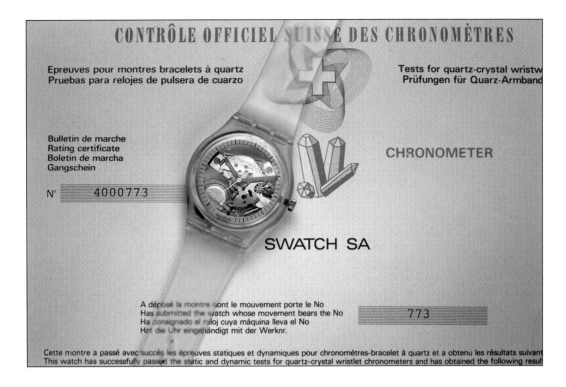

### THE SWATCH CHRONOMETER:
·············· "NOT JUST A PRETTY FACE" ··············

From the start, Swatch proved that it was much more than just a frivolous fun watch. It showed that Swiss technology and expertise could be used for something visually exciting to all age groups which would also be inwardly as reliable and as sturdy as one of the heaviest stainless-steel sports watches.

Swatch put itself to the test and produced a run of 4,843 Swatches which were issued with chronometer certificates. These pieces were submitted to an amazing range of tests, including freezing temperatures, 90-degree humidity, and, not least, being left for twenty-four hours on a vibration machine. Obviously, with an issue of only 4,843 pieces worldwide, Swatch Chronometers do not often appear on the market, but their very existence is proof, if it were needed, of the company's commitment to maintaining quality regardless of price.

··························· MAXI SWATCH ···························

Swatch "sees big" with a Swatch measuring more than 6 feet (6 feet 6¾ inches, to be precise). Designed to be hung on a wall in the home or office, it is a piece of furniture, but the company went further still with the largest Swatch ever made – it weighs 13 tons and is 548 feet long.

ABOVE **Swatch Chronograph: Signal flag (SCN 101).**

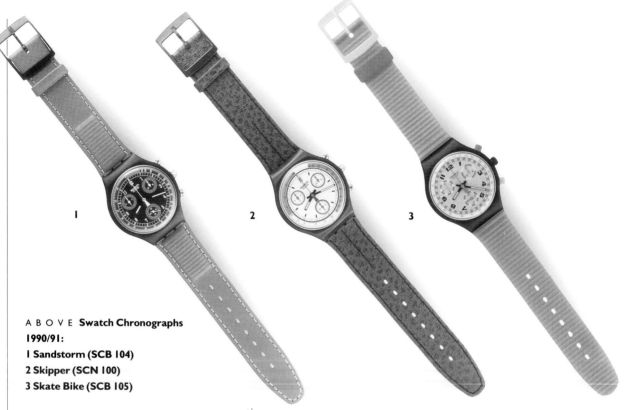

A B O V E **Swatch Chronographs**
**1990/91:**
**1 Sandstorm (SCB 104)**
**2 Skipper (SCN 100)**
**3 Skate Bike (SCB 105)**

A B O V E **One More Time: GU (H) RKE PWZ 100. BONJU (H) R PWZ 101 and VERDU (H) RA PWZ 102, Pop Swatch Art, 1991.**

## POP SWATCH

The Pop Swatch is an outsize watch that pops off its strap, which is also very large. This is yet another success story, both in its ordinary form and as one of the Pop Swatch Art series or Christmas Specials. The Pop Swatch strap was designed to fit over the sleeve of a coverall, an idea generated by the old aviator watches. A further development in this model is the medium version, larger than an ordinary Swatch, but smaller than a standard Pop Swatch.

## SWATCH MECHANICALS

Although Swatch was launched as the ultimate in simplified quartz movements, when a renewed interest in mechanical movements became apparent, the company brought out its automatic wrist watch. First available in 1991, it is both shock- and water-resistant. The mechanical Time to Move model bears the logo of the Earth Summit held in Rio de Janeiro in 1992.

## SWATCH CHRONOGRAPH AND STOP SWATCH

The year 1990 saw the arrival of the Swatch Chronograph, a highly sophisticated movement with four stepping motors, yet with a case the same size as that of the ordinary Swatch. The watch became available with a leather strap in 1991. The Swatch Chronograph

A B O V E **The two Swatches shown in full are the SDK 100 deep blue SDN 400 Bora Bora and Swatch Scuba 200, 1990/1991.**

A B O V E **Foundation Maeght Series: GZ 110 by Polbury, GZ 111 Valerio Adami, and GZ 401 by Pierre Alechinsky, Swatch Art, 1988.**

offers functions to record finishing time and intermediate time and a tachometer for speed indication. The early chronographs are much sought and should form part of any Swatch collection. The company has gone further with the Stop Swatch: the first push on the button sends the hands back to twelve o'clock, and another push starts a stopwatch with a six-hour range.

#### ·········· SWATCH SCUBA ··········

Capable of withstanding depths of up to 650 feet, the Swatch Scuba has a timing bezel with very brightly colored, clear numerals to facilitate legibility. The models have mainly nautical names such as Captain Nemo and Sea Grapes.

#### ·········· SWATCH PAGER/PIEPSER ··········

One of the latest brainchildren of the Swatch engineers, this is another first – the world's first wrist watch with a built-in radio receiver. Its electronics necessitate 1,290 square feet of silicon, compared with 38 square feet for an ordinary Swatch. There is an antenna under the crystal which picks up signals from one of four predetermined callers. The next generation of this Swatch will have a liquid crystal display which will be able to show the number of the caller.

RIGHT **Lady Limelight and Sir Limelight (LB 110 and GB 106), 1985.**

ABOVE **Zoo Loo, Chicchirichi (GR 112), Swatch, 1992, Spring/ Summer.**

ABOVE **Vivienne's Pop Swatch. 1992 Fall/Winter PWK 168 Putti by designer Vivienne Westwood.**

If you collect Swatches, the permutations are clearly endless. Not only have they produced limited editions, special and singles, but also whole series by major contemporary artists: for instance, the Pop Swatch Art Series, One More Time, by Alfred Hofkunst, which includes three models. The firm's first art watch (which has recently been sold at auction for a very large sum of money) was the 1985 Kiki Picasso. This was followed in 1986 by a series by Keith Haring featuring four pieces. The year 1987 was represented by the Folon Series together with Tadanori Yokoo. In 1988 there was the Foundation Maeght Series by artists such as Pol Bury, Valerio Adami, and Pierre Alechinsky. The Mimmo Paladino 1989 Art Swatch has been quoted as selling for up to $25,000. However, before embarking on a search for such elusive pieces, it may be more practical to set your sights a little lower and concentrate on some of the early singles.

If you decide to become a Swatch collector, you will be joining a worldwide club with over 130,000 members. Its own newspaper, *The Swatch Journal*, aims to transmit information to club members as speedily as possible. Club members are offered special Swatches available only to them which are not sold through normal outlets. The company also makes available to members an annual catalog to bring them up to date on the four regular launches: spring, summer, fall and winter.

RIGHT **Christmas in Vienna: Mozart (GZ 114), Swatch Specials, 1989.**

ABOVE **Christmas: Hollywood Dream (GX 116), Swatch Specials, 1990.**

ABOVE **700 years Swiss confederacy, 360 degrees (GZ 119) by Rosso Su Blackout, Swatch Art, 1991.**

The Swatch creators did not set out to start a trend, but Swatch mania has prevailed since the early days, and each new product launch has been greeted with such enthusiasm that, in some cases, supply has been far outstripped by demand. The reasons behind all this are simple enough – Swatch has an excellent product selling for the right price and a marketing team capable of taking it into realms so far not thought of by anyone else. Moreover, the watch's bright colors and affordability appeal to younger people, its reliability attracts the purist who wants a highly precise timekeeper, and the sportsperson is also catered for with chronographs and diving watches. Finally, because Swatch's popularity has snowballed (even in the art world, thanks to the Art Specials), there are now models kept in glass cases in museums – which, for a watch which started out as an inexpensive "second watch," is truly an achievement.

# TIPS FOR COLLECTORS

Big towns, little towns, even small villages have jewelry stores which sell both old and new wrist watches. Do not hesitate to ask if they have anything else apart from the goods displayed, for untold treasures have been dug out of dusty boxes lying dormant at the back of even dustier storerooms.

······················· HOW TO BUY ·······················

Another way to see a variety of pieces and to buy the more collectible item is to visit an auction room. Articles to be sold can be viewed before the sale, and auction house catalogs can be a valuable source of information. There is a myth that you need only yawn at an auction to find subsequently that you are the proud owner of a very expensive and totally unwanted object. Auction sales these days are regulated affairs with well-trained and, for the most part, friendly and approachable staff, who are only too glad to help and answer questions. If you go to one of the major auction houses, they will even be able to tell you what will be going on sale in their branches on the other side of the world!

It is important to keep an open mind when bidding for a particular watch. Do not forget that you may not be the only person interested in it, and never stay in the bidding for longer than you meant to! Local taxes and auction house charges (generally between 10 and 15 percent) are added on top of the price reached

A B O V E **These Longines watches are interesting because of the device that blocks the outer bezel to allow for accurate adjustment of the time.**

in the bidding. This should be kept in mind to avoid nasty shocks when it comes to paying for your purchase.

As a collector, you will want to keep your collection alive. One way to do this is to use part-exchange as a method of purchase: many dealers and retailers will make an allowance for this. If you have decided that a wrist watch, for whatever reason, does not belong in your collection, put it aside for part-exchange. When you have spotted another piece which you feel does belong, take your old wrist watch along and see whether the seller will lower the price of the watch that you want if you leave your watch as part of the deal. It is assumed, of course, that you will be trading up to obtain a more desirable item than the one you are leaving behind.

### ··········· WHERE TO GO FOR INSPIRATION ··············

In order to buy intelligently and to keep your collection growing, you need information and facts – after all, to collect is to be constantly learning. There are watch collections in one form or another in most major towns, where both public museums and private collections are good sources of information. Many countries, including the U.S., France, Germany, and Britain, have contributed to make the watch industry one of the most fascinating and changing, and there are tangible records of this across the world.

Many watch manufacturers have their own private collections which may be seen by appointment. The Longines headquarters in St. Imier, Switzerland, for example, has its own private museum which houses some pieces of historical importance and goes right back to the origins of the brand. Visiting both private and public collections will help you to decide which way you want your collection to go, and which theme or topic you wish to follow. There is a list of useful addresses on page 79 of this book. In addition to those listed, many museums with twentieth-century design departments will feature wrist watches in their collections.

### ················ MAKING A GOOD PURCHASE ················

Once you have decided where to buy and what to buy, there are a few points to remember when purchasing a vintage wrist watch. If you are going to wear the watch, it must be capable of telling the time; if it is not, it must be returned to working order. With a quartz watch, it may be just a matter of replacing the battery, but

A B O V E **When browsing through stores and auction houses, be alert: this innocent-looking bangle has an early Rotary watch concealed inside.**

A B O V E **This watch is over fifty years old, but the cleanliness of the movement shows that the previous owners have taken good care of it, making it a safe purchase.**

A B O V E **Limited editions are normally indicated on the watch itself. For example, this piece is no. 15 out of a total production of 300.**

B E L O W **The importance of documentation. Limited editions are very often logged at the manufacturer's headquarters where the ownership of each piece is carefully noted.**

bear in mind that a service and overhaul may add considerably to your overall outlay in purchasing a watch.

If a mechanical wrist watch is not in working order, there could be a multitude of reasons. If a ticking sound can be heard when the watch has been wound but the hands are not moving, it is possible that the hands have come away from the dial train (the wheels and pinions of a watch). Not every wrist watch, especially an early one, was made shock-resistant, and the hands may have become disconnected after a severe knock. This is not a major problem and can be rectified by a competent watch repairer.

However, if there is complete silence, if the watch cannot be wound or if there is a "grinding" feel when you try to wind it, things could be decidedly more serious and, again, the possible repair costs must be taken into account when considering purchasing the watch.

········ THE IMPORTANCE OF DOCUMENTATION ········

When you buy a new watch, you should be issued with the appropriate box, a valid guarantee, a full set of instructions matching the movement of the watch (unless the operation of the watch is so basic that you do not need instructions), and, most important of all if the watch has the word "chronometre" on the dial, you should be given the certificate proving that it has passed stringent chronometer testing.

When purchasing a secondhand item, remember that the more valuable and rare the item, the more documentation will add to its value. The original guarantee, stamped by the original retailer, together with the right box can add a great deal of money to the asking price.

Whether buying old or new, beware of the difference between a limited edition and a special edition. In principle, it is easy to remember. As part of a limited edition for which only a relatively small number of watches have been produced, the watch will carry a number: this number is individual to the watch. A special edition will possibly be a commemorative piece or a production tied to some sports event, with no set number but with, perhaps, a note as to the commemoration on the back.

## ········ How To Care For Your Collection ········

Mount your collection of wrist watches on rolls made of soft fabric or acid-free tissue paper, if they do not have their own boxes.

Never leave dead batteries in quartz watches. If a mechanical wrist watch stops, have it serviced immediately. Find a good watch repairer early in your collecting career and stay with him or her – you will learn a lot. Watch repairers can be fascinating people to talk to, with a wealth of professional expertise to draw upon.

Your collection will need cleaning from time to time. This refers to the outside only: never attempt to clean, oil, or regulate the movement or change the battery yourself; always leave any dealings with the inside of a watch to a professional watch repairer. To clean the case of most metal watches, a soft cloth is all that needs to be used. Certainly never use solvents on gold plate or silver gilt. Silver watches may be rubbed gently with an appropriately impregnated cloth. If the water resistancy has been confirmed, the metal part of a wrist watch may be cleaned in soapy water and dried with a soft fiberless piece of fabric.

## ······ Checking For Damage Before Buying ······

Examine the watch with a magnifying eyeglass. Do not forget to check the strap or bracelet as well: if you are buying the watch to wear, it will not stay on your wrist for long if the pins (lugs) are bent or if the stitching, in the case of a leather strap, is worn.

Although several grades of leather are used for straps, the most water-resistant being sharkskin, you are not likely to find the original leather on a vintage watch. Obviously, the finer the watch,

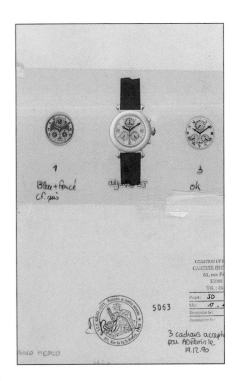

**A B O V E  In great houses such as Cartier, each design is carefully numbered and registered from the initial concept to the finished product.**

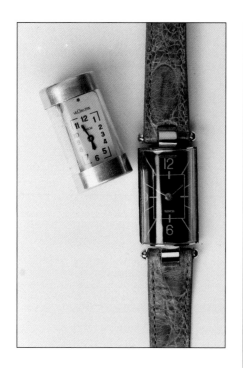

A B O V E **1930s Duoplan by Jaeger-LeCoultre, the watch with an accuracy outstanding even in the 1990s.**

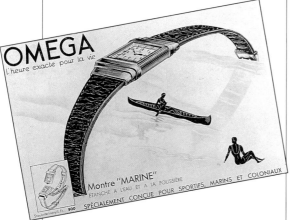

A B O V E **Sign of the times: in this 1930s advertisement for an Omega sports model, the watch was promoted as being suitable for sportsmen, sailors, and "colonials"!**

the better the grade of leather the strap would have been initially. However, be it boarskin, ostrich skin, calf, crocodile, or lizard, if you wet a leather strap on a regular basis, it will deteriorate that little bit quicker, and the harder you intend to wear the watch, the stronger the strap needs to be. In fact, for frequent sports use a metal bracelet is best; otherwise, resign yourself to buying a new leather strap on a fairly frequent basis. After all, if you regularly dunk a pair of shoes in water, they won't last long either!

One problem to look out for with regard to metal bracelets is stretching. If the links seem very far apart with large gaps between them and a lot of "play," the bracelet needs professional attention. If it is made of gold, the metal may have become worn, and the lugs inside the links may also be worn or distorted.

A watch with a machine-made gold bracelet will be less expensive than one with a mainly hand-assembled loose-link type. The problem likely to occur with these machine-made bracelets after a number of years is splitting: this can be repaired by a competent goldsmith, but the repair always shows, and the split will recur in a different position if the bracelet is at all stressed.

················ FURTHER COLLECTING TIPS ················

### ORGANIZING YOUR COLLECTION

Each piece in your collection should have its own file containing its photograph, the date and place of purchase, any important serial and model numbers, and information regarding related pieces. The photograph will be invaluable should it become necessary to insure all or part of the collection, and serial numbers can help trace a provenance. This file should also contain any guarantees or chronometer certificates issued by the watch manufacturer.

### LEARNING MORE ABOUT WATCHES

In addition to books on wrist watches, there are also collectors' magazines which provide detailed information about featured models. When you visit a watch retailer, do not forget to ask for the current catalogues of any brand that takes your interest. Much can be gained from having a small, well-ordered library of such literature, including news releases, historical facts, details of technological improvements, and so on. It can also be interesting to ask the auction houses for their sale-room catalogs after an

## COLLECTING THEMES

A B O V E **Dinotime and Fantasea watches for children by Flik-Flak. These are water-resistant watches made from recycled materials with appealing designs.**

auction, with a list of prices achieved: this will keep you up to date on desirable prices and give you some idea of the value of your own collection.

## COLLECTING BY THEME

Most "young" wrist watch collections represent a mixture of styles, manufacturers, and themes. As your collection grows and you learn more about the subject and what you do and do not like, your purchases are likely to become more specialized, and the watches will fall naturally into categories or themes which you can then expand upon. The themes around which you can collect are many and varied, and you should not be restricted to collecting by, for example, manufacturers alone. The earlier chapters of this book will have given you some ideas already, and a few more are suggested on this page.

## CHILDREN'S WATCHES

An interesting – and less expensive – collection can be formed from novelty and children's watches. The first watch specifically aimed at children was made in 1933 by Ingersoll and featured Mickey Mouse; since then, a wide range of images and designs have been introduced.

Flik-Flak, a Swiss company, has an excellent selection ideal for starting a collection. Young children are well catered for with Flik-Flak's teaching watches, and the company also offers a good range of pictorial models featuring dinosaurs and seahorses. The watches are made from recycled aluminum, have a canvas strap, and can be machine-washed at 100°!

There is also a large selection of character watches featuring faces well known the world over through comics, cartoons, popular television shows, films, and now computer games. An interesting collection could be formed by tracing the changing image of an old favorite, such as Bugs Bunny, through the decades.

Do not forget that children themselves enjoy collecting. There are many modern, brightly colored, and inexpensive wrist watches to suit the younger pocket. They will not have huge sums of money available for their collections, but think how many birthday and Christmas gifts are taken care of in this way. Researching and looking after a collection is great fun and a powerful teaching aid. Children (and adults!) take delight in swapping, which can be most useful when the allowance money runs out.

# A CHRONOLOGY OF WRIST WATCH INVENTION

| 19TH CENTURY | 1900–09 | 1910–19 | 1920–29 | 1930–39 |
|---|---|---|---|---|

**1838**
Louis Audemars invents stem winding and setting mechanism

**1868**

Patek Philippe makes the first wrist watch

**1871**
Aaros Dennison of the International Watch Company (IWC) invents the waterproof watch case

**1880**
Girard-Perregaux produces a wrist watch for officers of the Imperial Austrian Navy

**1888**

Cartier produces a lady's wrist watch with diamond and gold bracelet

**1902**

The first Omega wrist watch is produced

**1902**
93,000 wrist watches sold in Germany

**1903**
Louis Brandt, founder of Omega, dies

**1904**
One of the most famous early wrist watches appears – the Santos-Dumont produced by the House of Cartier

*Auguste Agassiz*

**1910**
Longines begins wrist watch production

**1911**
Santos-Dumont wrist watch goes on general sale

**1912**
Movado makes an army wrist watch with a protective grid over the glass

**1914**
First alarm wrist watch is made by Eterna

**1917**
British Royal Flying Corps issued with wrist watches by Omega

**1918**
Omega supplies US Army with wrist watches

**1920**

Audemars Piguet produces the smallest repeater watch (⅝ inch)

**1923**
Invention of the automatic wrist watch by John Harwood (the prototype is made by Blancpain)

**1925**
Patek Philippe produces the first wrist watch with a perpetual calendar

**1927**
First water-resistant Rolex Oyster produced

**1930**
Smallest lady's watch movement to date – baguette shaped – is produced

**1930**
Tissot develops the first antimagnetic wrist watch

**1932**
Launch of Reverso by Jaeger-LeCoultre

*Charles Lindbergh*

Manufacture of the Lindbergh Aviator by Longines (to a design by Charles Lindbergh)

**1933**
First watch for children made by Ingersoll (featuring Disney's Mickey Mouse)

Longines made official timekeeper at the Brazilian Grand Prix

**1936**
Omega appointed official timekeeper for the Olympic Games

| 1940–49 | 1950–59 | 1960–69 | 1970–79 | 1980–89 |
|---------|---------|---------|---------|---------|

**1940–49**

Hamilton supplies US services with wrist watches; Omega and Breitling supply RAF watches during the war years

**1945**
Rolex Datejust is the first watch with a date display on the watch face

**1946**
Audemars Piguet produce the thinnest wrist watch in the world (¹/₁₅ inch)

**1947**

American Nathan George Horwitt designs the Movado Museum Watch

**1950–59**

Poljot, the first Russian wrist watch, is produced – later to become Sekonda

Tissot develops Tissot Navigator, a self-winding wrist watch with a universal calendar

Rolex Submariner goes down 1,000 feet

**1952**
Breitling introduces the Navitimer, a super chronograph designed especially for pilots

**1953**
Lip's battery-powered watch is introduced

**1957**

Hamilton produces the first electric watch

**1960–69**

**1960**
Bulova launches Accutron, the electronic tuning-fork watch invented by Max Hetzel

**1966**
Girard-Perregaux produces the first high-frequency mechanical watch (36,000 vibrations per hour)

Creation of Beta I, the first Swiss quartz movement

**1969**
Girard-Perregaux develops the first mass-produced quartz watch

International Watch Company introduces the Da Vinci wrist watch

Longines produces the first quartz cybernetic wrist watch

Zenith brings back the El Primero, the epitome of chronograph movements

Neil Armstrong wears an Omega Speedmaster Professional on the moon

**1970–79**

**1972**
First stainless-steel luxury wrist watch is made (Audemars Piguet)

**1972**
Longines launches an LCD (liquid crystal display) watch

**1975**

Launch of Raymond Weil brand, with innovative ultra-slim movement

**1976**
Launch of Maurice Lacroix brand

**1978**
Vacheron Constantin Kallista is sold for $5,000,000

**1980–89**

**1983**
Swatch is launched

Rolex Sea Dweller goes down to 4,000 feet

Longines launches the Conquest line, accurate to about one minute in five years

**1985**

Tag-Heuer brand appears on the market

**1986**
Tissot brings out the Rock Watch

**1987**
Tissot introduces the TwoTimer (a watch showing both analogue and digital display)

# GLOSSARY

**ARABIC NUMBERS**
0, 1, 2, 3, 4, 5, 6, 7, 8, 9.
Originated in India and introduced by the Arabs to Europe in about the tenth century AD.

**ANALOG**
Time indication by hands and dial; means "corresponding." Originally an electronic term, it was adopted by watchmaking with the spread of the quartz watch.

**ANTIMAGNETIC WATCH**
Watch whose parts are protected from all but the very strongest magnetism; quartz watches cannot be disturbed by the phenomenon.

**APPLIED NUMERALS**
Raised metal characters attached to the dial.

**AUTOMATIC WATCH**
Mechanical watch with a mainspring that is wound by the wearer's movements, via a rotor. Invented by Abraham-Louis Perrelet in the eighteenth century; Breguet called his self-winders "perpetuelle."

**AUXILIARY DIAL**
Small dial showing seconds only, up to one minute, usually at the six o'clock position.

**BACK WINDER**
Flat crown set into the back of the case for setting time and winding.

**BAGUETTE**
Rectangular movement, with a length at least three times its width. Popular shape for Art Deco watches.

**BALANCE**
Running regulator of mechanical watch; it oscillates around its axis of rotation, the hair-spring making it swing to and fro ("tick-tock") in equal time parts. Balances of modern wrist watches beat up to ten beats per second.

**BARREL**
Circular box housing mainspring; teeth attached at edge drive gears; going barrel has great wheel mounted upon it.

**BATON NUMERALS**
Undecorated non-numerical markers of hours, minutes, and seconds.

**BEZEL**
Metal surround frame in which watch glass (crystal) is fitted.

**BREGUET HAND**
Popular design by Breguet; the slightly tapered needle of the hand ends in a pointed head mounted on a circle, which is pierced with a hole. Sometimes called a moon hand.

**BUTTON**
Better known as a crown, or winder; sometimes refers to a chronograph.

**CABOCHON CROWN (WINDER)**
Crown or winder set with a jewel.

**CALIBER**
Once used only to denote the diameter of a watch movement; now often only indicates type (i.e., men's, lady's, automatic). Generally given with manufacturer's name. From Latin *qua libra?* (of what weight?), or from Arabic *kalib* (mold, i.e., circumference, measurement, scale).

**CARAT**
The official scale by which the purity of the gold is determined. Pure gold is 24 carat; 18 carat is alloy in which 18 parts in 24 are gold; 14 carat contains 14 parts of gold, and so on. Also used as the unit of weight for precious stones.

**CASE**
The housing for movement, dial, and glass.

**CHRONOGRAPH**
Watch which also has an independent stopwatch for short interval timing. Common types are one-button (using crown, or separate button above it); two-button (the most common, the top button stopping and starting the time-measuring function and the bottom one resetting it); twelve-hour with moonphase; split-second.

**CHRONOMETER**
Ordinary watch which has passed extremely severe precision and reliability tests in an official (generally Swiss) observatory (such as Neuchâtel).

**COMPLICATED WATCH**

Watch with functions not related directly to the time of day (calendars, chronographs, moonphases, perpetual, repeaters, etc.).

**CROWN**

Knob, generally knurled and positioned outside the case at three o'clock, for winding, correcting, and setting.

**CRYSTAL**

Glass dial cover (in fact made of glass, plastic, synthetic sapphire, or quartz crystal), fitted into bezel. Plastic scratches; glass (common in pre-1940s watches) shatters easily; sapphire glass is virtually scratch-proof.

**DEPLOYMENT BUCKLE**

Two strips of hinged metal (curved to the wrist shape) on the watchband; upon closing, one folds over the other to cover it. Probably invented by Cartier.

**DIAL**

Face of watch, showing hours, minutes, and seconds. Other small dials are called subsidiary dials.

**DIVER'S WATCH**

Water-resistant.

**DOCTOR'S WATCH**

Also known as a duoplan or duodial. An auxiliary seconds dial is separate from the hour and minute dial; useful for quick reference when taking a pulse count.

**FORM WATCH**

Watch in any very unusual shape.

**GOLD**

Yellow, pink, or white, used for cases and bracelets.

**HACK FEATURES (BALANCE STOPPING)**

Second hand which is stopped to synchronize time, when crown is pulled out.

**INTEGRAL BRACELET**

Designed as a natural extension of watch case.

**JEWELS**

Used as bearings at points of greatest friction in movements; commonly fifteen to eighteen are used (the quantity is not indicative of either quality or value of watch). Formerly, natural rubies and sapphires were used; today most such jewels are synthetic.

**LUG**

Part or parts of watch case to which band, bracelet, or strap may be attached.

**MAINSPRING**

Principal spring in watch; a flat spring is coiled in a barrel.

**MEAN TIME**

Average length of all solar days in year; the usual time shown by watches.

**MINUTE REPEATER**

Repeating watch that sounds hours, quarter-hours, and minutes.

**MONTH WINDOW**

Pierced opening in a mechanical digital watch displaying month, often abbreviated.

**MOONPHASE WATCH**

Watch displaying phase of moon through twenty-nine and a half days (correction for extra forty-four minutes per month often incorporated).

**MOVEMENT**

Complete mechanism of watch; from 120 to over 600 parts may be incorporated in it.

**OYSTER CASE**

Rolex watch with water-resistant case.

**PAVE**

Literally "paved with," as in dial with precious stones.

**PERPETUAL**

Self-winding automatic watch (see also AUTOMATIC WATCH).

**PERPETUAL CALENDAR**

Calendar mechanism with display which automatically corrects for long and short months and leap years. Formula adjustments for vagaries of the Gregorian calendar continue only until February 28, 2100; that is not a leap year, so manual changes will have to be made to all but the most complicated watches; likewise 2200, 2300, 2500, 2600, and 2700 will not be leap years.

**PLATINUM**

Precious silver-white metal, which is heavier than gold. Used for cases and bracelets.

**QUARTER-REPEATER**

Repeating mechanism which sounds hours and quarter hours.

**QUARTZ**

Rock crystal (silicon dioxide) that can be made to oscillate by electronic switching, maintaining its very constant frequency, in accordance with its cut. Synthetic quartz crystals are used today.

**ROLLED GOLD**
An extremely thin sheet of hot gold, pressed onto another metal; gold on watch cases is usually double thickness.

**ROMAN NUMERALS**
Besides Arabic, the most common numerals used on watch dials; note IIII instead of IV.

**ROTOR**
In automatic watches, the rotor winds the mainspring; in quartz watches, it is a permanently rotating magnet in the step-switch motor.

**RUBY**
The "ruby" referred to in watch-making today is, in fact, corundum, a synthetic stone. It is used to reduce wear on certain pivots.

**SAPPHIRE**
Glasses (crystals), sold as scratchproof, are made of synthetic sapphire.

**SHOCK-RESISTANT WATCH**
A watch is held to be shock-resistant if, when dropped onto a hardwood surface from a height of 3 feet it does not stop, or if its daily rate does not change by more than sixty seconds.

**SIGNED MOVEMENT**
The signature on a movement of its maker, which is likely not to be the same as that on the dial.

**SKELETON WATCH**
The dial of a skeleton watch has a separate chapter ring with the interior cut away, leaving only numerals and exposing the wheels and the interior mechanisms of the movement. The back plate is also cut away and fitted with glass.

**SPLIT-SECOND CHRONOGRAPH**
Chronograph with sweep second hand, independent of chronograph hand.

**STEM**
Shaft connection between winding mechanism and crown on outside of case.

**SUBSIDIARY DIALS**
Smaller auxiliary dials, which show elapsed minutes and running seconds.

**SWEEP SECONDS (CENTER SECONDS)**
Second hand mounted at dial center and extending to chapter ring.

**"SWISS MADE"**
A Swiss Federal government ordinance dated December 23, 1971 decrees that this expression can only be featured on a watch and used in connection with its marketing if (a) at least 50 percent of the components, by value, excluding costs of assembly, are of Swiss manufacture, (b) it was assembled in Switzerland, (c) it was started up and regulated by its manufacturer in Switzerland, and (d) it is continuously subject to the legal obligation of technical inspection in Switzerland.

**TACHOMETER**
Speedometer or revolution recorder on bezel.

**TANK CASE**
Today, the common name for a rectangular case; originally, exclusive name of Cartier wrist watch.

**TONNEAU**
Case shape with wide center and flat tapered ends.

**TOURBILLON**
Invention by Breguet for nullifying vertical position errors by means of a revolving platform which goes through all such positions, so that they neutralize each other.

**TRITIUM**
Luminous paint for dials, hands, and numerals.

**TUNING FORK**
A transistor continually switching between two small magnets to regulate smooth running, oscillating 360 times a second. The high frequency gives great precision in timekeeping. Bulova Accutron made the use of the device famous, but then quartz watches usurped its popularity.

**WATER-RESISTANT**
Expression for "waterproof," which is illegal in the U.S. Water-resistant watches, sold as such, must be able to withstand water pressure at a depth of 3¼ feet for 30 minutes and thereafter for 90 seconds at 65 feet. Divers' watches in fact have much greater resistance.

**WORLD TIME WATCH**
A watch that can be made to depict current time in any chosen city or zone, according to the model.

# USEFUL ADDRESSES

## BRITAIN

The Antiquarian Horological
Society
New House
High Street
Ticehurst
East Sussex
TN5 7AL

Bonhams
Auctioneers
Montpelier Street
Knightsbridge
London SW7 1HH

British Horological Institute
Upton Hall
Upton
Newark
Nottinghamshire
NG23 5TE

Christie's
Auctioneers
8 King Street
St. James
London
SW1Y 6QT

Phillips
Auctioneers
Blenstock House
7 Blenheim Street
New Bond Street
London W1Y 0AS

Sotheby's
Auctioneers
34-35 New Bond Street
London
W1A 2AA

International Watch Magazine
Hyde Park House
5 Manfred Road
London
SW15 2RS

## USA

Christie's
Auctioneers
502 Park Avenue
New York
NY 10022

National Association of Watch and
Clock Collectors Inc.
514 Poplar Street
Columbia
Pennsylvania 17512-2130

Sotheby's
Auctioneers
1334 York Avenue
New York
NY 10021

The Time Museum
7801 East State Street
PO Box 5285
Rockford
Illinois 61125-0285

## SWITZERLAND

Christie's
Auctioneers
8 Place de la Taconnerie
1204 Geneve

Musee d'Horlogerie
Chateau des Monts
CH-2400 Le Lode

Musee d'Horlogerie et de
l'Emaillerie
Route de Malagnou 15
1208 Geneve

Musee International d'Horlogerie
Rue des Musees 29
La Chaux-de-Fonds

Sotheby's
Auctioneers
13 Quai de Mont-Blanc
CH 1201 Geneve

Swiss Watch and Jewelry Journal
International Edition
25 Chemin du Creux-de-Corsy

# INDEX